The Price Waterhouse
Personal Tax Strategy

1995 EDITION

Doubleday Canada Limited

Personal Tax Calendar

This Personal Tax Calendar shows key **tax deadlines**, indicating the day of the month for 1995. (Some dates change slightly from year to year.) The calendar also raises **planning reminders** that may need consideration.

To avoid missing deadlines or valuable planning opportunities, **check this calendar periodically**. You may want to add your own tax-related dates and planning reminders.

January

Deadlines

★ 15 Fourth U.S. estimated tax payment for prior year
🍁 30 Interest on employee and family loans (p. 13)
🍁 31 Inform employer of personal use of car
★ 31 File U.S. tax return if owed estimated tax on January 15 but did not pay (to avoid penalty)

Planning reminders

🍁 Contribute $6,000 of periodic payments to spousal RRSP? (p. 28)
🍁 Contribute to RRSP – for last year and this year? (p. 26)
🍁 Superficial loss? (p. 105)
🍁 Use Home Buyers' Plan (p. 209)

February

Deadlines

🍁 14 Reimburse employer for personal automobile expenses

Planning reminders

🍁 Expecting a tax refund? File early. (p. 193)
🍁 Slips and receipts to assemble?
🍁 Need year-end for new business? (p. 63)
🍁 Review and update your will? (p. 212)
🍁 Use Home Buyers' Plan (p. 209)

May

Deadlines

Planning reminders

🍁 Contribute to RRSP? (p. 26)
🍁 Superficial loss? (p. 105)
🍁 183 days in Canada this year? (p. 44)
🍁 Review and update your will? (p. 212)
🍁 QSSP strategy formulated? (p. 124)

June

Deadlines

🍁 15 Second tax instalment (p. 78)
★ 15 Second US tax instalment
★ 15 US tax returns, or 2-month extension request due (US citizens living in Canada and non-resident aliens not subject to withholding)
🍁 30 Bonus from own corporation? (p. 75)
🍁 30 Non-resident rental property (sec. 216) returns
★ 30 Non-resident special payment (sec. 217) returns (e.g., alimony, pension)

September

Deadlines

🍁 15 Third tax instalment (p. 78)
★ 15 Third US estimated tax payment

Planning reminders

🍁 Superficial loss? (p. 105)
🍁 Contributing to charities or political parties? (p.172)
🍁 CNIL problems to eliminate? (p.101)

October

Deadlines

★ 15 US Individual tax returns – last day for filing if you obtained a 2-month extension from August 15

Planning reminders

🍁 Contribute to RRSP? (p. 26)
🍁 Affected by changes in recent budgets? (p.8)
🍁 Moving soon? (p. 20)
🍁 183 days in Canada this year? (p. 44)
🍁 CNIL problems to eliminate? (p.101)

The symbols beside each deadline or planning question indicate the relevant jurisdiction.

🍁 Canada   ⚜ Quebec only   ★ U.S.   ● International

March

Deadlines
🍁 1   RRSP contribution in respect of prior year (except in leap years) (p. 26)
⚜ 15   First tax instalment (p. 78)
⚜ 31   Trust returns and preferred beneficiary elections (30th in leap years)

Planning reminders
🍁   Expecting a tax refund? File early. (p. 193)
🍁   Slips and receipts to assemble?
🍁   Superficial loss? (p. 105)
🍁   Affected by changes in recent budgets? (p. 8)

April

Deadlines
★ 15   US tax return or 4-month extension request due, or file for extension for non-resident aliens (subject to withholding)
★ 15   First US estimated tax payment
★ 15   US Trust and Partnership Returns or 3-month extension request due
🍁 30   File tax return (p. 193)

Planning reminders

July

Deadlines
★ 15   U.S. Trust and Partnership returns – filing deadline if automatic 3-month extension obtained.

Planning reminders
🍁   Superficial loss? (p. 105)
🍁   Claiming capital gains exemption? (p. 72)
🍁   Moving soon? (p. 43)
🍁   Objecting to a notice of (re)assessment? (p. 196)

August

Deadlines
★ 25   U.S. Individual tax returns – last day for filing if you obtained a 4-month extension

Planning reminders
🍁   Need year-end for new business? (p. 63)
🍁   Review and update your will? (p. 212)
🍁   Contribute to RRSP? (p. 26)

November

Deadlines
🍁 1   Canada Savings Bonds

Planning reminders
🍁   Superficial loss? (p. 105)
🍁   Need year-end for new business? (p. 63)
🍁   Claiming capital gains exemption? (p. 208)
🍁   CNIL problems to eliminate? (p. 101)
⚜   Any QSSP transactions required? (p. 124)

December

Deadlines
🍁 15   Fourth tax instalment (p. 78)
🍁 31   Expenses to claim (p. 68)
🍁 31   RPP contributions (p. 24)
🍁 31   RRSP conversion at age 71 (p. 132)
🍁 31   Car operating benefit election (p. 36)
★ 31   Fourth state estimated tax payment for deduction in year just ending

Planning reminders
🍁   Contributing to charities or political parties? (p. 172)
🍁   CNIL problems to eliminate? (p. 101)
⚜   QSSP strategy complete? (p. 124)

Contents

A detailed table of contents appears
at the beginning of each chapter.

Developing Your Personal Tax Strategy

Using this book — special features

This book has several features to make personal tax planning easier. It has a chapter especially for you if you are:

- an employee;
- an owner/manager;
- separated or divorced or
- an investor;
- retired;
- a taxpayer with U.S. connections.

Issues that could affect all taxpayers are covered in chapters on:

- 1994 highlights;
- calculating your taxes;
- filing returns and paying your taxes; and
- looking ahead.

Each chapter has a distinctive graphic icon. Throughout the book, **international aspects** are marked by a stylized globe. Numerous tax tips highlight valuable tax-saving techniques. An **Index** is also provided.

A **detailed table of contents at the beginning of each chapter** helps you find topics that interest you.

Québec taxpayers have to deal with not only the federal system but a substantially different provincial tax regime. At the end of each chapter, a special **Québec section** sets out tax matters that are significantly different in that province.

Key tax numbers are collected in **appendices**. Graphs and tables present information in an easily digestible form in the appendices and throughout the text. The **Personal Tax Flowchart** on pages 167 and 177 gives you the "big picture", revealing the components and structure of your income tax calculation.

2

Tax matters involve numerous acronyms such as AMT and CNIL. A **glossary** at the end of this book decodes common tax abbreviations (page 240).

You'll find the **Personal Tax Calendar** before the table of contents of this book. Referring to your Personal Tax Calendar several times throughout the year will remind you of tax planning opportunities as well as important deadlines.

Developing Your Personal Tax Strategy

Your personal tax strategy is important. This introductory chapter outlines steps you should consider to begin your tax planning, and explains the features of this book that can help you.

Why develop a personal tax strategy?

Investing time in your personal tax strategy can help you minimize your taxes, both short-term and long-term. You may be able to cut your tax bill by:

- reducing the amount payable this year; and

- deferring payment until a later year.

Cash flow management is part of a good personal tax strategy. The success of your tax plan, whether it is basic or complex, may be undetermined if you do not give enough consideration to cash flow issues.

Make sure that you refer to the chapter Filing Returns and Paying Your Taxes (page 188). You may find that you can save some money, or at least improve cash flow, by applying some of the simple tactics described in that chapter, both at tax time and throughout the year. For example, managing your instalment payments or reducing the tax withheld from your pay cheque may leave you with more discretionary income with which to implement some of your tax strategies - or just to save or spend.

This book will show you the many advantages of tax planning. Now may be a good time to get started.

4 | Getting the most out of this book

You can use this book to:

- reduce your tax bill by identifying tax planning opportunities to implement yourself or with professional advice;

- understand the process of preparing your income tax return, whether you do it or have it done for you; and

- save time and money by answering many of your questions and focusing your attention.

Beginning your tax planning

To begin your tax planning:

- Review your 1993 returns and assessments to help you recall the sources of your income and the deductions you have claimed.

- Note extraordinary transactions, events or amounts for later consideration and possible special action.

- Estimate your 1994 taxable income by calculating your income and deductions, using your 1993 return and this book as guides (see "Calculating your taxes" page 163).

- Check your liability for tax instalments. If your tax deductions at source do not cover most of your total tax liability, you may be required to make quarterly instalments. If you are required to make instalments of tax, Revenue Canada should already have sent you notices for each of your four 1994 instalments. You may pay your instalments according to this system, or, you may use the method you have used in the past. As long as you base your instalments on the Revenue Canada notices and pay your instalments on time, you won't be charged interest and penalties, even

To get the most out of Personal Tax Strategy, don't wait until your tax return is almost due before looking through it for tax planning opportunities – start now. Use whatever approach works best for you: flip through the pages, scan the table of contents or start with the Personal Tax Calendar before the table of contents. Then zero-in on material that applies to you.

if your payments fall short of your total tax liability for the year. If you missed any instalment payments that were required during the year, you can minimize charges by making a catch-up payment now. (See page 192.)

• On the Personal Tax Calendar (before the table of contents), mark any dates and planning points that apply to you. On your own calendar, mark a few reminders to review the Personal Tax Calendar. Use this book to identify planning techniques and to help you assess tax saving opportunities.

• Balance the cash flow requirements of possible deferral techniques against the potential for reduced tax.

• If you disagree with the re-assessment for 1993 or a prior year, dispute it by discussing it with Revenue Canada and perhaps by filing a Notice of Objection (see page 196). A disagreement can invalidate the amounts for your quarterly instalments specified in Revenue Canada notices.

After completing your analysis, consider discussing your conclusions with a professional advisor.

Use it throughout the year

Personal Tax Strategy is a planning tool, so you may want to refer to it several times throughout the year. That's why we suggest marking a few dates in your own calendar. On those dates, a glance at the Personal Tax Calendar will remind you of important tax-related deadlines and planning opportunities.

Use it at tax time

When the time comes to prepare your tax return, Personal Tax Strategy will help you understand how the various entries are related and why they are calculated the way they are. Personal Tax Strategy complements the tax guides that Revenue Canada provides, which help you with the details of filling out your return.

Beyond this book

This book is no substitute for competent professional advice. Tax planning is a complex process that must be tailored to your circumstances. Accordingly, the comments and advice in this book are not intended to be a definitive analysis of the law, but rather to guide you in understanding some of the ways to minimize your tax burden.

Throughout Personal Tax Strategy you will encounter references to the 1994 federal and provincial budget proposals, as well as to other draft legislation and technical amendments. How should you deal with rules that are still just proposals or draft? Usually, you should assume that these measures will become law, whether they give or take away your opportunity to do something.

If you are considering implementing a complex tax plan, or when significant amounts are involved, you should consult your professional advisor before proceeding.

Effective dates for implementation are provided wherever particular changes or proposals are discussed.

This book is based on:

- legislation enacted up to the end of September 1994;

- Department of Finance Press Releases announced up to September 30, 1994;

- Bill C-17, tabled on March 16, 1994, incorporating measures announced in the February 22, 1994 federal budget;

- proposals in provincial budgets. (All provinces had presented their 1994-95 budgets when Personal Tax Strategy was written.); and

- the Protocol to amend the Canada – U.S. Tax Convention, signed on August 31, 1994.

Post-publication changes in the interpretation of the law or in the Department of National Revenue's administrative policy could affect the information in this book.

Additional information on any of the matters discussed in Personal Tax Strategy is available from any Price Waterhouse office in Canada. See the back pages of this book for addresses.

1994 Highlights

To assess your overall personal tax position, you should review the changes that come into effect each year and understand how they could alter your tax planning. The tax changes highlighted below, along with their general implications, will help you see how you may be affected.

A number of personal tax changes introduced in the 1994 federal budget will affect your personal tax planning. In particular, the $100,000 lifetime capital gains exemption was eliminated for capital gains realized or accrued after February 22, 1994. A capital gain may still be sheltered by unused capital gains exemption in 1994 (see page 93). Capital gains realized on the disposition of qualified small business corporation shares and qualified farm property remain eligible for the enhanced capital gains exemption.

When the expression "enhanced capital gains exemption" is discussed or referred to in this book, the amount of the exemption will be taken to be $400,000. This assumes that the general lifetime capital gains exemption has already been claimed. For individuals who have not used their $100,000 capital gains exemption in respect of other property, the enhanced exemption will be $500,000.

The provinces left personal income taxes virtually untouched in their 1994 budgets. You may still be affected by changes announced in last year's provincial budgets, however. A number of provinces introduced both tax rate and surtax hikes that came into effect at the beginning of 1994. For example, the two levels of surtax in Ontario are 20% and 30% (up from 17% and 25% in 1993); British Columbia's surtaxes are 30% and 50% (up from 20% and 30% in 1993); New Brunswick's tax rate jumps from 62% of federal tax in 1993 to 64% in 1994; and the Yukon tax rate for 1994 is 50%, up from 48% in 1993.

The appendices provide more detail on income tax rates.

Tax change	Implications for you
As noted above, many 1993 provincial budgets introduced increased tax rates and surtaxes that took effect in 1994.	If you pay tax in British Columbia, New Brunswick, Ontario, Nova Scotia or the Yukon, you may face a higher provincial tax bill in 1994.
There is a small "hidden" federal tax increase for 1994, because the tax brackets and your personal and other credits will be the same in 1994 as they were in 1993.	The tax brackets and credits increase from one year to the next to the extent that the increase in the Consumer Price Index exceeds 3%. While the good news is that inflation was less than 3%, if your income increased by at least the rate of inflation, you will face a higher tax bite.
The 1994 federal budget proposes to subject the age credit to an income test.	The amount on which the age credit is based will be reduced at a rate of 15% of net income in excess of $25,921. The reduction will be phased in over two years. If you lose the entire credit your combined federal and provincial income taxes will increase by about $475 for each of 1994 and 1995. (The actual amount will depend on your province of residence.)
Measures announced in the 1994 federal budget will eliminate the $100,000 lifetime capital gains exemption.	Generally, you will no longer be able to shelter capital gains realized after February 22, 1994 with the capital gains exemption. If you have capital gains exemption available and own capital property with accrued gains, however, you may be able to shelter the portion of the gain that accrued up to budget day. An election must be filed with your 1994 income tax return.
Proposals introduced in the 1994 federal budget will extend taxation to the first $25,000 of coverage under an employer-provided group term life insurance policy.	Your combined federal/provincial tax will increase by between $15 and $25 in 1994 and between $30 and $50 in 1995 (the actual amount will depend on the benefits under the plan as well as on your province of residence).

Higher tax bills

Tax change	Implications for you
Lower tax bills The tax credit for charitable donations will increase slightly beginning in 1994.	Your combined federal/provincial tax bill will decrease by about $15 for 1994 and subsequent taxation years.
Retirement savings The federal budget proposes to continue the RRSP Home Buyers' Plan, scheduled to end on March 1, 1994, for first-time home buyers only.	If you are a first-time home buyer, the modified Plan means that you may be able to purchase a home much sooner than you would have been able to otherwise. The withdrawals must be repaid to your RRSP in instalments over 15 years. Amounts not repaid will be included in your income and taxed accordingly.
Tax shelters A proposal in the 1994 federal budget may require a negative adjusted cost base in a partnership interest to be included in a partner's income as a capital gain.	If you invest in a tax shelter that is structured as a partnership, you may have to report as a capital gain a negative adjusted cost base in that interest.
Other miscellaneous The deduction for tax purposes of business meals and entertainment expenses is further limited by proposals in the 1994 federal budget.	If you are self-employed, you will likely face a higher tax bill. Only 50% (down from 80%) of the cost of business meals, beverages and entertainment consumed or enjoyed after February 1994 will be deductible for tax purposes.
Changes to the instalment requirements for individuals became effective with the instalment that was due on September 15, 1994.	You must make quarterly instalments of tax if the difference between the amount of tax that is withheld at source and your tax payable is greater than $2,000 in both the current year and either of the two preceding years.
A Protocol that amends the Canada - U.S. tax treaty was signed. It will likely come into effect in 1995.	When the Protocol comes into effect, it will reduce some withholding rates, provide relief from tax treatment of cross-border pension and social security payments.

Employees

Employees

For most employees, salary is the main component of income. Employment benefits are often a major component too. The T4 slip that your employer mails to you provides the tax information you need, and the tax consequences of salary are straightforward. Salary is generally taxed when received. However, if your salary is deferred and one of the main reasons is to postpone payment of tax, special rules impose tax on the amount deferred.

In addition to being an employee, you may also be a director, either of another corporation or of the corporation for which you work. If you are a director and are earning directors' fees, those fees are also considered to be employment income and must be included on your tax return. Directors' fees are "earned income" for the purposes of determining how much you can contribute to your spousal RRSP. Refer to page 200 as well for a discussion concerning directors' liability.

Taxable benefits and employment deductions claim most of the attention. Company cars are a major topic on their own, and are dealt with on page 32. Other taxable benefits, nontaxable benefits, and employment deductions (including pension, RRSP and DPSP contributions) are covered first.

Taxable benefits

You must include the value of any taxable benefits received during the year as a result of employment in your income from employment. The most important taxable benefits are company cars, employee loans, and stock options. Frequent flyer points also deserve some attention.

The 1994 federal budget proposes to include in an employee's income coverage under an employer-provided group term life insurance policy. Prior to the budget announcement, the first $25,000 of coverage was not considered to be a taxable benefit.

		Prescribed rate for deemed interest on employee and shareholder loans*
Quarter of 1994	1st	5%
	2nd	4%
	3rd	6%
	4th	7%

* For prescribed rates for overdue taxes, penalties, refunds. etc. see the table on page 63.

Employee loans

Generally, if your employer makes a loan to you or to a member of your family and charges little or no interest, you receive a taxable benefit. The benefit is computed as the interest on the loan at a prescribed rate, less any interest you actually paid within the year or 30 days after year end. The table shows the 1994 prescribed rates for these loans. Rates are subject to adjustment every quarter to reflect market interest rates.

If you use the loan proceeds for investment purposes, the loan may be essentially tax-free, since the benefit is offset by an interest expense deduction equal to the amount of the benefit.

The taxable benefit on a loan to acquire a home that you will occupy, or to refinance a mortgage on your current home, is calculated using the lesser of the prescribed interest rate in effect at the time the loan was made or renewed, and the current prescribed rate. These loans are considered to be renewed every five years.

Tax Tip

If you expect interest rates to rise, it may be worthwhile arranging for your employee home purchase loan to be renewed for a further term. The lower rate of interest will be locked in and the resulting taxable benefit will remain constant for five years. Because of the way the prescribed rate is calculated, you will know in advance if it will increase in the next quarter.

14

Tax Tip

If you started work at a new job in Canada that involved moving within Canada to a home at least 40 kilometres closer to your new work location, the interest benefit on the first $25,000 of a home relocation loan will be tax-free. This exemption is available for the first five years of the loan.

Stock options

Stock options that you get from your employer are taxed differently depending on whether or not the corporation is a Canadian-controlled private corporation (CCPC). In either case, you face no immediate income tax consequences when you receive an employee stock option.

If your employer is not a CCPC, when you exercise an option you are deemed to have received income from employment equal to the difference between the fair market value of the stock when the option is exercised and the total amount you paid to acquire the option and the shares themselves. You may deduct one-quarter of this deemed benefit from your taxable income, so long as the options are qualifying stock options granted after February 15, 1984. Consequently, just three-quarters of the benefit on the exercise of these options will be taxable as employment income.

A stock option qualifies if the exercise price for the share is not less than its fair market value when the option is granted, the employee deals at arm's length with the corporation, and the shares under the option arrangement are common shares meeting specific criteria.

The first criterion is applied without reference to fluctuations in the value of a foreign currency relative to the Canadian dollar during the period between the acquisition of the option and the time the share is acquired. Accordingly, when the stock options are denominated in a foreign currency, the deduction will not be denied by reason only of a foreign exchange fluctuation.

On a subsequent sale, three-quarters of any gain accruing after the exercise date is treated as a taxable capital gain.

Stock options granted to employees of CCPCs are not subject to tax until you dispose of shares. When you dispose of shares in a CCPC, the difference between the fair market value of the shares at the time the option was exercised and the total amount you paid to acquire the options and the shares themselves is treated as employment income. One-quarter of this amount is deductible in arriving at taxable income, provided you have held the shares for at least two years. As with options in non-CCPCs, three-quarters of any gain on the sale accruing after the exercise date is treated as a taxable capital gain.

Draft legislation that enacts 1994 federal budget proposals will eliminate the $100,000 lifetime capital gains exemption for gains realized or accrued after budget day. Accordingly, if you sold shares in 1994 but prior to budget day (February 22) and some or all of your capital gains exemption is still available to you, you may offset a capital gain realized on the disposition with the exemption. Further, if you sell shares after budget day that you acquired under a stock option plan, or if you own shares with accrued gains that you acquired before budget day, you may shelter capital gains that accrued up until February 22, 1994 to the extent that you haven't used your lifetime exemption. To use the exemption you will have to make an election in your 1994 income tax return. Refer to page 93 for further details. Gains on sales of stock in a qualifying small business corporation (QSBC) acquired by exercising options are still eligible for the additional $400,000 capital gains exemption.

When unexercised options under an employee stock option plan are held on the date of death of a taxpayer, an employment benefit equal to the difference between the fair market value of the options immediately before the employee's death and the amount paid by the employee to acquire the options will have to be included in the taxpayer's final income tax return.

Tax Tip

In general, decisions to invest or sell should be based on economic factors, with tax considerations secondary. However, in some cases clear tax advantages should be taken into account. For example, your shares of a CCPC acquired as a result of exercising a stock option prior to May 23, 1985 should be sold before selling your other securities. There will be no taxable benefit and the full gain is a capital gain. While the $100,000 lifetime capital gains exemption has been eliminated, a capital gain may still be sheltered by unused capital gains exemption in 1994 (see page 93); gains realized on the disposition of QSBC shares remain eligible for the enhanced capital gains exemption.

Tax Tip

If you borrow to finance the purchase of shares when exercising stock options, the interest expense on the loan is tax deductible. The interest expense will, however, be added to your cumulative net investment losses (see page 101).

Frequent flyer points

If you accumulate frequent flyer credits while travelling on business trips paid for by your employer and then use the points for yourself or your family for personal air travel, Revenue Canada requires you to determine and include in your income the fair market value of any benefits enjoyed. If your employer did not control the program, it is your responsibility to calculate and report the benefit.

While salaries, wages, commissions and other remuneration paid to employees are not subject to the GST, fringe benefits or perks may be. Some of the more common perks that are included in your income as taxable benefits and that are subject to GST are:

- personal use of your employer's automobile;

- short-term board and lodging (less than one month);

- the cost of tools, certain gifts, and frequent flyer programs;

- tuition fees for GST-taxable courses; and

- noncash incentives such as prizes, awards and holiday trips that are GST-taxable in the marketplace and that are provided as benefits to employees.

GST will not apply to prizes or awards given to employees in the form of cash or a cheque.

Employers who are not registered for GST generally do not have to remit the GST on employee benefits. However, the GST element of taxable employee benefits must still be included in an employee's income for tax purposes.

Nontaxable benefits

Many employees receive other forms of compensation as well as those discussed already. Known as fringe benefits or perquisites ("perks" for short), a dwindling number of these noncash benefits are received tax-free. Here are some examples:

- employer contributions to registered pension and deferred profit sharing plans (within limits);

- reimbursement of moving expenses;

- employee counselling services (including tobacco, drug or alcohol counselling, stress management counselling and job placement and retirement counselling) provided by or paid for by the employer;

- tuition fees for courses taken for the employer's benefit;

- employee discounts (within limits);

- subsidized meals, provided the employee is required to pay a reasonable charge;

- distinctive uniforms and special clothing (including safety footwear);

- use of employer's recreational facilities (except board and lodging at a vacation property such as a summer hotel or hunting lodge);

- social or athletic club memberships that are advantageous to the employer;

- reimbursement of a loss on the sale of a home due to an employment transfer;

- reasonable allowances for taxi fares, "para-transport" and parking provided to employees who are eligible for the disability tax credit by reason of a severe and prolonged impairment of mobility or sight; and

- allowances for attendant care required to enable an employee who qualifies for the disability tax credit to perform employment duties.

Employee relocation reimbursements

A job transfer could require you to move from one city to another within the same province, or across the country. Depending on the location and timing of a move, an employee could incur significant additional costs to acquire a home comparable to the one left behind. As part of an employment package, many employers compensate employees for higher housing prices in the new work location.

Two recent court decisions dealt with payments to employees in partial reimbursement of increased costs in new locations. In one case, the Federal Court of Appeal overturned the decisions of the lower courts and found that the taxpayer had to include the payments received from his employer in his employment income as a taxable benefit. The facts in the second case, currently under appeal, are quite similar.

Essentially, a distinction was made between relocation payments that compensate employees for increased housing costs in a new location and for losses suffered on the sale of a previous home. The case affirms the taxability of payments for relocating to a more expensive location and the exemption from tax of relocation payments that reimburse an employee for actual losses incurred on a sale.

Tax Tip

If, as a result of a job transfer, you received a relocation payment in a prior year that is not statute-barred and you excluded the amount from income, you should reconsider the circumstances to determine whether the exclusion is still justified. It would be prudent to discuss your situation with your professional advisor. (The taxpayer in the case referred to above has appealed the Court's decision. If the appeal proceeds, a further review of the situation will be necessary when it is decided.)

Tax Tip

If you will be relocating in the near future, consider suggesting that your employer review, and possibly restructure, the company's relocation program to ensure the most effective tax treatment. For example, while payments for defraying higher costs at a new work location, including payments for the incremental interest cost of assuming a new mortgage with both a higher interest rate and a higher principal amount, appear to be taxable, the reimbursement of increased mortgage interest payments resulting from an employer-initiated move may not be.

Employment deductions

The Income Tax Act is not generous in permitting deductions in the computation of employment income. Only those expenses specifically included in a short list are deductible. Some of those with more general application are discussed below.

Moving expenses

Eligible moving expenses incurred in connection with beginning employment or full-time postsecondary education at a new location in Canada are deductible if your new residence is at least 40 kilometres closer to your new work or school location and if the expenses are not reimbursed by your employer. Eligible expenses are deductible only from income earned at the new location. Amounts not deducted in one year may be carried forward to the next year.

Eligible moving expenses include travelling costs for you and your family, including a reasonable amount for meals and lodging; moving and storage costs for your household effects; the costs of cancelling a lease or selling the old home; and legal costs of purchasing a new home.

A reimbursement of reasonable moving costs by your employer is not considered a taxable benefit. On the other hand, you cannot deduct costs that the employer reimburses.

Tax Tip

Since provincial tax is based on your province of residence on December 31, a higher than expected tax liability may arise with a move to another jurisdiction. If this will be the case, consider postponing your move until after the year end. On the other hand, consider accelerating the move if you are moving to a province with a lower tax rate.

Legal expenses

You may deduct legal costs paid to collect salary or wages from your employer or former employer. Legal expenses paid to collect or establish a right to a retiring allowance or pension benefit are deductible within a seven-year carryforward period in computing income for the year in which the allowance or benefit is received. The deduction is limited to the amount of retiring allowance or pension benefits you received, less any portion that has been transferred to an RPP or RRSP.

Tax Tip

If you incurred legal costs to collect pension income in the last three years, consider asking Revenue Canada to reassess your return for the period in question. Your tax refund could be significant.

Child care expenses

Working parents may deduct the cost of child care within specific limits. In most cases, the deduction must be claimed by the lower income spouse.

The maximum child care deduction depends on the child's age and any infirmity, as the table shows.

The maximum deduction is $5,000 for each child who is under seven years of age at the end of the year or has a severe or prolonged mental or physical impairment for which a Disability Credit Certificate has been submitted. The deduction is $3,000 for each child who is less than 15 years of age at the end of the year or who is not eligible for the $5,000 deduction but has a mental or physical infirmity and is dependent.

Child care expense: maximum deductions

			Child's age (at December 31)		
			15 or more	7 to 14	Under 7
	No Infirmity				
Mental or physical infirmity	Infirmity does not qualify for the $5,000 maximum deduction	Child not dependent on taxpayer or taxpayer's spouse	None		
		Child is dependent on taxpayer or taxpayer's spouse		$3,000	
	Severe and prolonged impairment, for which a Disability Credit Certificate has been submitted			$5,000	

Eligible costs include day-care or babysitting, boarding school and camp expenses. Medical expenses, tuition, clothing or transportation expenses are not eligible for this deduction.

Tax Tip

For child care payments to be deductible in respect of the current year, they must be made by December 31. If you make January's payment in December, however, you are not permitted to deduct the amount until the following year.

Contributions to RPPs, RRSPs, DPSPs

Employees often accumulate funds to provide future retirement benefits through tax deductible contributions to a registered pension plan (RPP), a registered retirement savings plan (RRSP), a deferred profit sharing plan (DPSP) or some combination of these plans.

The rules that govern tax assistance for saving in pension and retirement savings plans are intended to ensure that individuals are treated equally, whether they save through RPPs, RRSPs or DPSPs.

While the rules are fairly straightforward if you save for your retirement solely through RRSPs, they can be complicated if you are a member of an RPP or a DPSP. The Pension Adjustment (see below) determines what portion, if any, of the maximum RRSP contribution is replaced by benefits accrued under an RPP or a DPSP. The maximum amount you can contribute to your RRSP must then be reduced accordingly.

• Pension Adjustment (PA)

Simply put, your Pension Adjustment (PA) measures the benefits accrued to you as a member of a pension plan. The maximum you will be allowed to contribute to an RRSP is reduced by your PA.

The way the PA is calculated depends on the type of pension plan:

The PA (pension adjustment) calculation

	Type of plan		
	DPSP	RPP	No pension
	Money purchase	Defined benefit	
PA	Total employee and employer contributions in the year (generally)	Complex calculation intended to measure value of benefits accrued in the year	None

In a money purchase plan, the pension you receive depends on the investment earnings of the pension fund. In a defined benefit plan, pension payments are independent of the fund's earnings, depending instead on a formula that usually involves a percentage of your average earnings and your period of pensionable employment.

Your employer is responsible for determining your PA. Your T4 slip for 1993 employment earnings will tell the amount of your PA. You will have to reduce your RRSP limit by the prior year's PA. Revenue Canada will also advise you of your 1994 RRSP deduction limit on your 1993 Notice of Assessment or late in 1994.

24

If you are a member of a foreign pension plan, you may still have a PA. For example, if you are resident in Canada, but work primarily outside Canada, you may be required to calculate your own PA-like amount with respect to any foreign plan to which you belong. In other circumstances, it will be your employer's responsibility to calculate and report your PA. The PA calculations can be very complex. If you are concerned about whether your PA has been calculated and reported correctly, consider having your tax advisor discuss the matter with your employer.

To complicate matters further, something called a Past Service Pension Adjustment (PSPA) may result if, for example, your pension plan is retroactively upgraded to provide better benefits or if you transfer benefits to a new plan and purchase additional past service benefits. If you have a PSPA, the amount that you may contribute to your RRSP will require adjustment. Once again, the onus is on your employer to provide you with the necessary information regarding these very complicated rules.

RRSP contribution limits may be reduced by your PA and PSPA

Not a member of an RPP or a DPSP	A member of an RPP or a DPSP
Full RRSP contribution limit (see table on page 26)	**PA** (pension adjustment)
	PSPA (past service pension adjustment)
	Reduced RRSP contribution limit

• Registered pension plans (RPPs) – money purchase

If you belong to a money purchase RPP, you may make a tax-deductible contribution to your plan in 1994 equal to 18% of your 1993 employment income, to a maximum of $14,500, minus the contribution your employer makes to your plan (see the table on page 26). You reach the $14,500 maximum when your employment earnings are $80,556.

The RPP money purchase limit will increase to $15,500 in 1995. **25** The limit is to be indexed after 1995 to reflect increases in the Canadian average industrial wage.

• Registered pension plans (RPPs) – defined benefit

Generally, the amount you may contribute to a defined benefit RPP and deduct for tax purposes is not limited, as long as the contributions are in respect of current service and are required under the provisions of the plan. However, the government caps the amount of pension an individual may receive, and the provisions of your RPP will ensure that the restrictions are met by limiting how much you and your employer can contribute. Maximum contributions relate to the maximum benefit that can be accrued, which in turn is based on a maximum annual pension allowed in the first year of retirement. That maximum pension equals your years of pensionable service, multiplied by the lesser of:

- 2% of the average of the best three consecutive years of salary; and

- $1,722 (indexed from 1996 to the year of actual retirement).

Maximum pension (per year of pensionable service)

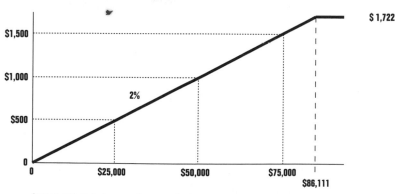

Average of three best consecutive years of salary

As the graph shows, the $1,722 cap corresponds to an average of $86,111 for the best three consecutive years of salary.

26 | **• Registered pension plans – additional voluntary contributions (AVCs)**

AVCs are contributions made under a money purchase provision of an RPP that are not required as a general condition of membership under the plan. Even in a defined benefit RPP, AVCs generally provide benefits on a money purchase basis. (However, if voluntary contributions are made to purchase defined benefits, the PSPA rules discussed earlier must be considered). AVCs are permitted as long as the Pension Adjustment limits (see page 23) are not exceeded.

Retirement savings contribution limits

		RRSP	DPSP	RPP Money purchase	Defined benefit
		(Limits to be reduced by the PA and PSPA for members of RPPs or DPSPs)	(Employer's contributions only)	(Limits apply to total employer and employee contributions)	
Fixed dollar limit*	1992	$12,500 (if income > $69,444*)	$6,250 (if income > $34,722*)	$12,500 (if income > $69,444*)	No direct limit (Contributions governed by actuarial principles and specific rules.)
	1993		$6,750 (if income > $37,500*)	$13,500 (if income > $75,000*)	
	1994	$13,500 (if income > $75,000*)	$7,250 (if income > $40,278*)	$14,500 (if income > $80,556*)	
	1995	$14,500 (if income > $80,556*)	$7,750 (if income > $43,056*)	$15,500 (if income > $86,111*)	
	1996	$15,500 (if income > $86,111*)	Indexed		
	After 1996				
Income-based limit (all years)		18% of previous year's earned income	18% of employment income		

* Below the given level of income, the 18% limit applies rather than the fixed dollar limit.

Prior to October 9, 1986, past service AVCs could be made under certain circumstances. If this type of AVCs were made, have not been deducted and were annuitized as retirement income, up to $3,500 a year may be deducted against post-1986 retirement income.

• Registered retirement savings plans (RRSPs)

An RRSP is a tax-deferred investment vehicle that allows you to invest money now, with a view to using the accumulated funds as retirement income commencing not later than the end of the year in which you turn 71. Your contributions are tax deductible within specified limits. If you borrow money to make an RRSP contribution, the interest payments are not tax deductible.

As the table above shows, your RRSP contributions for 1993 cannot exceed 18% of your earned income for the previous year, up to a dollar limit of $12,500 (which corresponds to $69,444 of earned income). If you are a member of an RPP or a DPSP, these limits are reduced by your:

- pension adjustment (PA) for the previous year, described on page 23;

and

- past service pension adjustment (PSPA), described on page 24.

The RRSP limit of $13,500 for 1994 will increase by $1,000 per year until it reaches $15,500 in 1996. The limit is to be indexed after 1996 to reflect increases in the Canadian average industrial wage.

To be deductible in a particular year, your RRSP contributions must be made before the end of the year or in the first 60 days of the following year. Beginning in 1991, if you do not make the full RRSP contribution that you are entitled to, the balance can be contributed and deducted for income tax purposes without limitation over a period of at least seven years (including the year to which the unused RRSP contribution room relates). The amount of unused RRSP contribution room that can be carried beyond the seven years is restricted.

Remember that earned income does not include any type of periodic retirement or pension payment or benefit, including retiring allowances, death benefits and amounts received from an RRSP. In addition to your regular RRSP contribution, you may transfer a retiring allowance to your RRSP to the extent of $2,000 per year of service, plus $1,500 per year of service before 1989 during which you were not a member of an RPP or DPSP.

28 **• Spousal RRSP contributions**

Contributions to a spousal RRSP based on your contribution limit are deductible from your income. These contributions, however, reduce the amount you can contribute to your own plan for the year.

You can also contribute, tax deductible, up to $6,000 of pension income from an RPP or DPSP to your spouse's RRSP for 1994, the last year this special contribution is available.

You can continue to contribute to your spouse's RRSP until he or she is 71, even if you have already reached that age. In addition to gaining access to the pension income credit, receipts from a spousal RRSP may help equalize the amount of retirement income you both receive, and may place you in a lower tax bracket.

Tax Tip

Don't get trapped by a timing rule associated with withdrawals from a spousal RRSP. If you withdraw amounts from a spousal RRSP, you, rather than your spouse, will have to include the withdrawals in your income to the extent that you paid the tax-deductible premiums into the spousal plan in the year or in the immediately preceding two taxation years. Many people make the mistake of thinking of RRSP contributions as having been made in the year they are deductible, rather than in the year they were made. For example, a contribution made in February 1994 and deducted on your 1993 tax return will be included in your income and taxed on your return if the amounts are withdrawn before 1997, i.e., within two years of the time when the contribution was made.

• Over-contributions to an RRSP

You will pay a penalty if you exceed your total RRSP contribution limit by more than $8,000. The penalty is 1% per month of your "cumulative excess amount" (the amount of the over-contribution above $8,000) at the end of the month. The $8,000 over-contribution threshold is not available if you are under the age of nineteen.

If you over-contribute (perhaps because of lower-than-expected earned income), you may end up paying double tax, i.e., you don't get a deduction for tax purposes for the excess amount and you will pay tax on the amount when it is eventually withdrawn as retirement income. You can, however, avoid paying double tax: when you receive your Notice of Assessment for the year in which the excess arose, you may withdraw that excess amount tax-free, in:

• the year of the over-contribution;

• the year you receive the assessment; or

• the year immediately following either of those years.

If the over-contribution is intentional, you lose the ability to make a tax-free withdrawal.

Even though you have this opportunity to withdraw the excess amount tax-free, you will still be liable for the penalty tax if the over-contribution exceeds $8,000. If your over-contribution was due to a reasonable error, you can ask Revenue Canada to waive the penalty tax.

Tax Tip

You might still consider over-contributing to your RRSP by up to the $8,000 limit if you were going to invest this sum outside an RRSP in any event. Investment income earned on the over-contribution will not be taxed and you have the option of deducting the over-contribution at any time as long as you have RRSP contribution room available.

For example, assume that you have enough earned income to claim the maximum RRSP deduction and that you contribute $21,500 to your RRSP in 1994: the maximum of $13,500 for 1994, plus $8,000 of over-contribution. In 1995, you are eligible to con-tribute the maximum for that year as well, which is $14,500, but you only have sufficient cash to contribute $6,500. You can claim a deduction on your 1995 tax return for the entire $14,500: your cash contribution of $6,500 in 1995, plus $8,000 of over-contribution from 1994.

Be careful if you decide to implement this strategy: ensure that your over-contribution does not exceed $8,000 or you will be subject to the 1% per month penalty.

• Deferred profit sharing plans (DPSPs)

A deferred profit sharing plan (DPSP) can be used in lieu of an RPP. A DPSP is an arrangement under which an employer makes payments – for example, a percentage of annual profits – to a trustee. The trustee holds and invests the contributions for the benefit of employees who are plan members.

Tax-deductible contributions may be made to a DPSP by your employer. As the table on page 26 shows, the contribution for 1994 is limited to the lesser of 18% of your remuneration and $7,250. The limit will increase to $7,750 in 1995. Beginning in 1996, the $7,750 limit will be indexed in the same manner as the maximum RPP contribution limits (of which the DPSP limits are one-half). Employee contributions to DPSPs are not permitted.

Amounts withdrawn from a DPSP are taxable, but in determining the taxable amount, you may deduct the contributions that you made to the plan.

You may transfer lump sum proceeds from a DPSP into an RPP, an RRSP, or another DPSP, generally tax-free.

• Individual pension plans (IPPs)

An important objective of the sweeping changes to the rules governing tax assistance for retirement savings was equality between RPPs and RRSPs. That goal, however, could not be fully realized. For example, a well-designed defined benefit RPP can, in certain circumstances, provide greater tax-assistance than an RRSP.

To allow taxpayers to take advantage of this opportunity the Individual Pension Plan (IPP) was developed by Price Waterhouse. An IPP is essentially a defined benefit RPP that is specifically designed to provide the maximum benefits that can be funded prior to retirement. As the name suggests, each IPP has only one member, which permits flexibility to meet each individual's circumstances. The IPP also shares similarities with defined contribution arrangements, such as RRSPs, in that all funds in the plan belong to the member and will be used to provide benefits to the member or heirs. The IPP is a feasible option for an individual who is over the age of 38, earns at least $82,000 in 1994 and expects earnings to grow at least as fast as the average industrial wage.

This is a complex area and professional advice is a must. You will need competent assistance to assess the potential benefits of a plan to you, and, if an IPP is indeed appropriate to your particular circumstances, to establish the IPP itself.

Other expenses

Annual dues required to be paid to a professional body, a trade union or similar body are generally deductible. Office rent, salary paid to an assistant, and the cost of supplies that an employee is required to pay under an employment contract may also be deductible.

If your office is part of a house or apartment that you rent, you

Home office expenses – employees

Deductible (if conditions are satisfied*)	Not deductible
Rent and maintenance attributable to the office. Maintenence expenses include: – fuel – light bulbs – electricity – minor repairs – cleaning materials	– capital cost allowance – mortgage interest
Commissioned sales people only may deduct a portion of these expenses: – taxes – insurance	

* Expenses are deductible only if the workplace is:
• your principal place of employment; **or**
• used by you both:
  – exclusively for the purpose of earning employment income; **and**
  – "on a regular and continuous basis" for meeting customers or other persons in the course of employment.

may be able to deduct certain home office expenses, as the table shows, as long as the required conditions are met.

Home office expenses can be deducted only up to the amount of your employment income for the year. To the extent that you cannot use the full deduction in a particular year, you may carry forward work space expenses indefinitely and deduct them from employment income in future years.

Reduced employee withholdings

(See page 188 – Interest-free loans to the government?)

Tax Tip

If your taxable income will be substantially less than the amount your employer uses to calculate the tax to withhold, possibly as a result of extraordinary deductible expenses that you have incurred, write to your district taxation office requesting a reduction. (You may want to discuss this with your professional advisor first.)

Employees and automobiles

The taxation of automobile benefits and expenses has always been complex. If you own your car, reasonable distance-based allowances for your costs will not be included in your income; other allowances may be. If you received a taxable allowance, you may be able to deduct some of the actual expenses you incurred.

Automobiles – taxable benefits

If your employer provides you with an automobile (as defined in the *Income Tax Act*), you are considered to have received two types of taxable benefits: a standby charge (which reflects your access to the car) and an operating cost benefit (which reflects the personal portion of such expenses that are paid for by your employer).

If your employer provides you with a motor vehicle that is not an automobile, you are still considered to have received taxable benefits (i.e., a personal use benefit and an operating cost benefit), but these benefits are calculated differently than the benefits described below. For more information, contact any Price Waterhouse office in Canada.

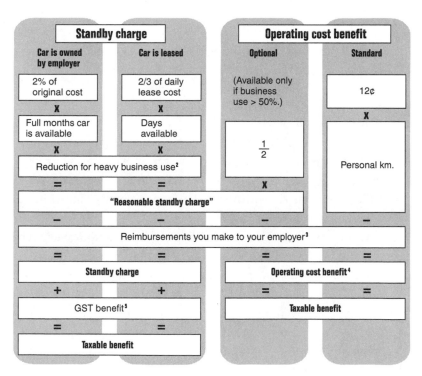

Standby charge		Operating cost benefit	
Car is owned by employer	**Car is leased**	**Optional**	**Standard**
2% of original cost	2/3 of daily lease cost	(Available only if business use > 50%.)	12¢
X	X		
Full months car is available	Days available		X
X	X	$\frac{1}{2}$	
Reduction for heavy business use[2]			Personal km.
=	=	X	
"Reasonable standby charge"			
−	−	−	−
Reimbursements you make to your employer[3]			
=	=	=	=
Standby charge		Operating cost benefit[4]	
+	+	=	=
GST benefit[5]		Taxable benefit	
=	=		
Taxable benefit			

1 Costs include PST, but not GST.

2 Reduction factor $= \dfrac{\text{personal kilometres}}{\text{1,000 kilometres x full months car is available}}$

   (Available only if business use is at least 90% and personal kilometres average less than 1,000 per month.)

3 Any operating costs reimbursed to your employer must be paid within 45 days after the end of the year.

4 Considered to already include a GST benefit component.

5 7% of "reasonable standby charge" recalculated excluding PST in original purchase cost or daily lease cost.

The standby charge is calculated differently depending on whether the employer owns the car or the car is leased, as the first two columns of the chart on page 33 indicate.

For purposes of calculating the standby charge, original cost and lease payments do not include the GST, but do include provincial sales taxes. See page 35 for an explanation of how the GST does affect taxable benefits relating to automobiles.

Tax Tip

The standby charge is calculated on the original cost of the car and does not decrease as the value of the car declines with age. After a few years, it may be cheaper to eliminate the standby charge by buying the car from your employer.

• Operating cost benefit

Changes to the calculation of the operating cost benefit for automobiles, effective for the 1993 taxation year, finally became law in 1994. The federal operating cost benefit formula is simply 12¢ × total personal kilometres (as shown in the chart on page 33). The 12¢ per kilometre rate will be reduced to 9¢ per kilometre for employees whose principal source of employment is selling or leasing automobiles. The reduced rate applies to 1994 and subsequent taxation years. The operating cost benefit is considered to already include a GST component.

Alternatively, if you use the car more than 50% for employment purposes, you can elect to calculate the benefit as half of the standby charge, less any amounts you reimbursed to your employer.

Under the proposals, the operating cost benefit is considered to already include a GST component.

Tax Tip

If your personal use is less than 50% of the total use and you prefer the alternative operating cost benefit calculation, you must notify your employer in writing before the end of the year.

Tax Tip

Minimize your personal use of an employer-provided automobile to reduce your operating cost benefit, and in some cases your standby charge benefit. There may be an advantage if you use your own car for personal purposes.

Tax Tip

Reimburse your employer for all personal use operating expenses within 45 days after the year-end to eliminate your operating cost benefit. If your employer has paid only a small portion of the operating expenses, consider repaying these amounts before February 14 of the following year so that you will not have a taxable benefit of 12¢ per personal-use kilometre for the entire year.

Tax planning measures may be available to reduce or avoid your operating cost benefit. Your arrangements should be evaluated to identify tax planning opportunities for reducing the benefit.

• Employer-provided automobiles and the GST

If your employer owns the car you use for business purposes, you must include in your income a standby charge based on the actual cost of the automobile, including provincial sales tax (PST). In addition, your taxable benefit in respect of the automobile must reflect the GST that relates to that portion of the purchase cost.

For example, the table below shows how the total standby charge that is added to your T4 slip includes $420 to reflect the GST component.

Standby charge in respect of:	employer's $25,000 car	($25,000 + $2,000 PST*) x 2% x 12 months = $6,480
	GST	25,000 x 2% x 12 months x 7% = $420
Total standby charge		$6,900

* Provincial sales tax (PST) is assumed to be 8% for this example.

N.B. The GST component must be added to the standby charge even if your employer did not pay GST on the purchase or lease cost of the vehicle.

The same applies to the standby charge for an automobile that is leased: the taxable benefit on a leased automobile must reflect two-thirds of the GST that would be applicable to the lease cost.

The amount of any operating cost benefit for an automobile already reflects an estimate of the GST your employer has paid on personal operating expenses.

For purposes of calculating the GST portion of the standby charge benefit, any reimbursement payment that you made to your employer in respect of the benefit is not to be taken into account.

Employee automobile expenses

If you use your own car in carrying out your employment duties, you will have a number of decisions to make. You will have to determine whether any amount you receive from your employer constitutes a reimbursement or an allowance; the tax consequences are different. You will then have to determine whether you are entitled to deduct any car expenses, and then how much.

• Reimbursements

A reimbursement is an amount that you receive from your employer to repay you for amounts (including GST) that you spent on your employer's business. Generally, you do not have to pay tax on a reimbursement unless it is a payment for personal expenses. An allowance, on the other hand, is a payment that you receive from your employer in addition to your salary and wages and that you need not account for. While the rules dealing with whether or not an allowance has to be included in your income are quite specific, some latitude is nonetheless permitted in applying them.

• Allowances

Essentially, an allowance must be reasonable for it not to be considered taxable to an employee. An automobile allowance is considered reasonable only if it is computed using an appropriate per kilometre rate that is applied to business driving by an employee. If you receive an allowance from your employer that is solely distance-based, it will ordinarily be considered to be reasonable and would not be taxable to you. Accordingly, your employer would not be required to withhold tax in respect of the allowance paid.

If the allowance is determined on another basis, it will not be considered to be reasonable and, therefore, will be taxable to you and subject to withholding at source. A taxable car allowance is not subject to GST. Since the allowance is included in your income, you may be able to claim reasonable business-related expenses.

If the allowance is distance-based and would otherwise be considered to be reasonable, but you believe that the allowance you receive is not reasonable because your business-related expenses exceed the amount of the allowance, you may choose to add the allowance to your income and claim reasonable business-related expenses. The onus is on you, however, to make this decision.

• Deducting automobile expenses

What's the bottom line? You may be permitted to deduct reasonable automobile expenses that you are required to incur in travelling to carry out your employment duties, so long as you are not reimbursed for the expenses and your employer does not pay you an automobile travelling allowance that was excluded from your income. You may deduct a portion of operating expenses, prorated according to the proportion that the distance driven in the course of employment is of the total distance driven. You are also entitled to a prorated portion of capital cost allowance (CCA), as well as leasing costs or interest on funds borrowed to buy the car, subject to certain limits.

If you deduct business-related car expenses on your personal tax return and your employer is a GST registrant, you may be eligible to apply for a rebate of the GST you paid. The rebate is not available if you choose to include an otherwise reasonable tax-free allowance in your income in order to claim business-related expenses.

	Maximum deduction*
Capital cost allowance (CCA) base	$24,000**
Monthly interest charges	$300
Monthly lease payments***	$650**

* For automobiles acquired or leases entered into after August 1989.

** Plus GST and PST on $24,000 and $650

*** Or lesser amount (determined by formula) for certain luxury vehicles.

Tax Tip

If you have two cars, consider using one exclusively for business and the other for personal use, to simplify record keeping.

Loss of employment

In today's weak economic environment, loss of employment seems to be more of a risk than ever.

In a plant closure, which may take place over a period of months or even a year or more, employees may be in a position to plan for coping with expenses, to re-arrange payment schedules for recurring obligations such as mortgages, and to seek other employment without urgency. When termination is unanticipated, however, perhaps because of downsizing or the takeover of an employer by another corporation, employees may find themselves in a difficult predicament, with the need to act quickly.

Little anyone does or says can mitigate the effect of loss of employment. There are, however, things you should be aware of and that you should consider in the unfortunate event that you find yourself without work.

Working with your employer is the first step in the process. While keeping costs down is a major concern, many of today's more enlightened employers are also concerned with providing employees with tax-favoured severance arrangements that do not result in an additional burden to the employer.

Sitting down with your spouse (and possibly other family members) and preparing a realistic budget and cash flow schedule is another critical element in this process. You need to determine exactly how much money you expect to be coming in and for how long, what your expenses are, which expenses you can defer and which you can cut entirely. If you anticipate a prolonged period of unemployment, don't wait until a major payment is due to the bank, for example, to let them know that you are unemployed. Schedule an appointment with your banker as soon as possible and try to re-arrange your payment terms.

Your re-employment counsellor (see below) should also be able to give you some suggestions on how to manage your financial position while you are looking for work.

The severance package

• Retiring allowances

The term "retiring allowance" may be a little deceptive because the definition encompasses a wide range of payments. A retiring allowance is an amount that you receive upon or after retirement from an office or employment in recognition of long service; or an amount in respect of a loss of an office or employment whether or not it was received on account or in lieu of payment of damages, or pursuant to a court order or judgement.

Your severance package may be determined by reference to your current remuneration, including benefits. While this may seem logical, the way in which your "golden parachute" is structured may prohibit you from making special tax-effective transfers to your RRSP or RPP (see below). Even though you no longer actually report for work, your severance arrangement may provide that in addition to amounts paid to you on termination, certain benefits of employment (medical and dental plan benefits and insurance coverage, for example) will also continue for a specified period. Because of the continuation of benefits, Revenue Canada may consider the payments you receive from your former employer to be employment income and not retiring allowances. Consequently, you may not be eligible to transfer these amounts to your RRSP or RPP.

• Transfer to RRSP or RPP

You may transfer all or a portion of your retiring allowance to your RRSP or RPP. The amount you may transfer is limited to $2,000 per year of service with your employer or a person related to your employer, plus $1,500 per year of service before 1989 in which you did not have a vested interest in contributions made by your employer to either a DPSP or an RPP.

While transferring as much as you are able to your RRSP or RPP is a tax-effective strategy, you must also consider your cash flow requirements. If you anticipate a prolonged period of unemployment, you may need to reduce the amount of retiring allowance to be transferred to your RRSP or RPP.

• RPPs

If you participate in your employer's RPP, you will have to determine what choices you have regarding contributions that you and your employer have made to your plan. If you are over a specified age and/or have a certain number of years of service with your employer, you may not be able to access funds in your RPP because you are "locked-in". If that is the case, you may have to wait until you are eligible to receive a retirement pension out of the plan, or you may only be able to transfer the funds directly into a locked-in RRSP or, when you begin new employment, to your employer's RPP if that plan provides for such transfers.

If you are not locked-in to your RPP, you may transfer the funds to your RRSP. If this transfer is done directly, then you need not suffer any withholding tax. On the other hand, if you need the funds immediately, your employer will have to withhold tax from the amounts to be paid to you and you will also have to include the

amounts in your income for tax purposes in the year you receive
them. Of course, any tax withheld at source will be credited to you
as a payment of tax.

You should contact your pension plan administrator for details
about your plan and the options you have for the funds accumulated
in the plan.

• Re-employment counselling/executive search services

As part of your severance package, your employer may provide you
with executive search services or the services of a professional re-
employment counsellor. Services of this nature that your employer
either provides or pays for are not a taxable benefit to you.

Tax Tip

When negotiating your severance package, consider having
your employer include re-employment counselling or executive search services. The counselling is generally very helpful,
and the considerable cost that your employer would incur to
provide you with the service is a tax-free benefit to you.

What if you disagree?

• Wrongful dismissal

The definition of retiring allowance is sufficiently broad to include
damage awards made by a court in an action for wrongful dismissal.
Accordingly, unless the facts indicate otherwise, an award for damages must be included in your income in the year you receive it.

Awards for damages to compensate for pain and suffering and
mental distress may, however, be non-taxable receipts, depending on
the facts and circumstances of the particular case. If you have sued
your employer for wrongful dismissal and the court has awarded you
damages, you should discuss the tax implications with your professional advisor.

• Legal expenses

You may generally deduct legal fees paid to collect or establish a right to salary or wages that are owed to you by your employer or former employer. Legal fees include amounts spent on negotiating your severance package as well as fees for litigation that becomes necessary.

While amounts that you receive as retiring allowances are specifically excluded from the definition of salary and wages, you may deduct legal expenses associated with retiring allowances, but with a limitation. The deduction is limited to the amount of the retiring allowance actually received in the taxation year that you did not transfer to your RPP or RRSP. For example, if your retiring allowance is $20,000, you transfer $15,000 to an RRSP and your legal expenses are $6,000, you may deduct only $5,000 of legal expenses.

Retiring allowances may be paid over a period of time. Since legal expenses may be deducted only to the extent of retiring allowances that you actually receive, Revenue Canada permits you to deduct legal expenses that you incur to collect retiring allowances over a seven-year period. This means that you can deduct a portion of your legal expenses against the retiring allowances that you receive each year in the carryforward period.

Continuity of benefits

• Loss of disability, medical, dental benefits, etc.

Many employers provide attractive benefit packages such as dental benefits for the employee and his or her family members, medical and travel insurance and disability insurance. While some severance packages may provide that these benefits continue for a short period after employment ceases, you should evaluate how you will replace these important elements of your compensation package and how much it will cost you to either get insurance coverage yourself, or to pay for services such as dental care out of your own pocket. Of course, if you have other employment lined up, this may not be a concern. If you anticipate a long period of unemployment, however, you should decide which types of expenses can be deferred and which services need to be replaced immediately.

Moving expenses

You may have to relocate to find new employment. If you move to a place in Canada that is at least 40 kilometres closer to your new work location than your old residence was you may claim eligible moving expenses, to the extent that they are not reimbursed to you by your new employer. You may deduct moving expenses only from income earned in your new capacity. If you move close to the end of the year, you may not have sufficient earnings against which to deduct moving expenses. In these circumstances, you may carry forward your moving expenses and deduct them the following year against income from your new employment.

Employees on temporary assignment

Many employee moves are only temporary. Employees may be moved for various reasons: to a head office for a one or two-year assignment; to fill a temporarily vacant position; to open a new office; or even to carry out a short-term assignment in a desirable location as a perquisite. A temporary period can be anywhere from a few weeks or months to five years.

For income tax purposes, one of the most important issues for employees either coming into or leaving Canada on a temporary assignment is their residency status during the period. Residence is a question of fact; the term "resident" is not defined in the Canadian *Income Tax Act*. The courts have held that an individual is resident in Canada for tax purposes if Canada is the place where he or she, in the settled routine of life, regularly, normally or customarily lives.

44   Until recently, Revenue Canada has been applying a general rule of thumb: unless the circumstances indicate otherwise, an individual who is absent from Canada for two years or longer would be considered a non-resident. The two-year rule notwithstanding, when an individual leaves Canada and takes up employment elsewhere, Revenue Canada is now taking the position that the individual is a resident of Canada during the entire period **if the individual has any intention of returning to Canada; for example, if there is a job waiting when he or she returns to Canada.** This appears to be the case even if otherwise all ties with Canada have been severed during the period the individual is out of Canada.

Revenue Canada considers a person who is present in Canada for two years or longer to be a resident for tax purposes.

An individual who sojourns (i.e., is temporarily present) in Canada for a total of 183 days or more in any calendar year is deemed by the Income Tax Act to be resident in Canada for the entire year. For this to occur, the individual must be a resident of another country during the 183 (or fewer) days in question.

Canada has bilateral income tax treaties with many countries. Where an individual appears to be a resident of Canada and another country, the treaties generally provide assistance through tie-breaker rules.

Depending on the circumstances, an individual's residency status and the time of taking up residence may be difficult to ascertain. A discussion with your professional tax advisor is strongly recommended well in advance of any move into or out of Canada.

In the comments below, it is assumed that employees temporarily in Canada are non-residents of Canada, and that employees on temporary assignment outside Canada remain Canadian residents throughout the period spent abroad.

Temporary assignments in Canada

If you are a non-resident of Canada, and you were employed in Canada at any time in the year or in a previous year, you will generally be subject to Canadian tax on your employment income and will be required to file a Canadian income tax return and a Québec income tax return if applicable. Depending on your country of residence, your employment income earned in Canada will probably be subject to tax in your home country as well.

The extent to which you will be able to obtain relief from double taxation will depend on whether or not foreign taxes are creditable against the income taxes levied under the laws of your country of residence, or whether there is a bilateral tax agreement between Canada and your home country.

The treaty rules regarding dependent personal services may provide relief from double taxation to individuals on international assignments. Generally, for remuneration received by individuals temporarily employed in Canada to be taxable in their home country only, the individuals must be present in Canada for less than 183 days and the remuneration must be paid by an employer that is neither a resident of Canada nor has a permanent establishment here. In addition, certain treaties set out a threshold amount of remuneration below which the host country (i.e., Canada) will not impose tax.

Temporary assignments outside Canada

The courts have held that everyone must be resident somewhere and that an individual can be resident in more than one place at the same time for tax purposes. If a resident of Canada goes abroad, but does not establish a permanent residence elsewhere, the presumption is that he or she remains a resident of Canada. Also, the fact that an individual establishes a permanent residence abroad does not by itself make the individual a non-resident of Canada. Where an individual is resident in Canada and, at the same time, resident in another country according to its laws, reference should be made to any tax convention or agreement that Canada may have with the other country.

46   A resident of Canada is taxed on his or her worldwide income. Accordingly, employment income earned during an assignment abroad will be subject to Canadian tax. The same income may, however, also be taxable in the foreign jurisdiction. Relief from double taxation will generally be available through either a tax treaty between Canada and the foreign country or the Canadian foreign tax credit provisions, or a combination of the two.

Tax Tip

If you are a Canadian resident during 1994 and have been or will be employed abroad for a period of more than six consecutive months that begins before the end of the year, you may be entitled to a tax credit designed to limit your Canadian tax liability. Generally, you must be employed by a Canadian resident, or a foreign affiliate of a Canadian resident, in connection with the exploration for or the exploitation of petroleum, natural gas, minerals or similar resources; or a construction, installation, agricultural or engineering activity. The credit, calculated annually, is determined by a formula that provides a tax reduction for overseas employment income that is less than $100,000.

Tax Tip

If you are considering a temporary assignment, and your employer has a tax protection or a tax equalization policy, you should become fully aware of the implications of the policy. Determine if you will be protected or equalized on employment-related income only, or on some or all of your income that is not related to your employment. This may be critical if you are earning significant non-employment income.

Giving up Canadian residence

If your departure from Canada constitutes giving up Canadian residence, you will be deemed to have disposed of all of your capital property (except taxable Canadian property; see definition below) at its fair market value at that date, and will be subject to Canadian tax on any capital gains. See page 93 for a discussion of the new rules regarding the elimination of the capital gains exemption.

Tax Tip

If you have taxable Canadian property that is a share of a QSBC or a qualified farm property and you have not used the enhanced $400,000 capital gains exemption, consider selling such properties with accrued capital gains to your spouse. In this way, you can use your enhanced capital gains exemption. This should be done prior to leaving Canada; if you dispose of the property after you have terminated Canadian residence, any capital gain will be subject to tax in Canada and you will not be able to shelter any of it with the enhanced capital gains exemption.

You will be required to file a part-year Canadian income tax return in the year in which you leave Canada. Ordinarily, you will report your worldwide income up to your date of departure. Additional Canadian tax liabilities could arise if you continue to carry on business or continue to be employed in Canada after you move away.

Canada's rules relating to a principal residence differ from those of other countries. If you intend to sell your home, your professional advisor can help you decide if you should dispose of it before or after you move. If you wish to rent out your home while you are away, you will be deemed to have disposed of it for proceeds equal to its fair market value, both when you convert your home to a rental property and when you reoccupy it as your principal residence. You may defer tax that would otherwise be payable on a capital gain arising as a result of the deemed disposition rules by electing for there to be no change in the use of your principal residence. Whether this election is beneficial to you will depend on how long you will be outside Canada and if you intend to return.

Prior to leaving Canada, you should discuss with your professional tax advisor the tax implications of exercising your Canadian stock options, of receiving payments from your former employer after you have left Canada in respect of services rendered in Canada, of interest earned in your RRSP, etc. The timing of your move will also be critical and will depend on the taxation year of the foreign country as well as on its tax rates compared with those in Canada.

Taking up Canadian residence

If you are taking up residence in Canada, you will generally be deemed to have acquired all of your capital property (except taxable Canadian property, defined below) at its fair market value on the date you take up residence. Any gain or loss on a subsequent disposition of that property will be calculated with reference to this deemed cost. Property acquired and disposed of after you become a Canadian resident will be based on the actual cost.

In the year in which you take up residence, you will be required to file a part-year Canadian income tax return. You will include your world income from the date of taking up residence in Canada, plus income that you received as a non-resident, to the extent that it relates to any business days spent in Canada in the year prior to the date you assume Canadian residence.

Tax Tip

Before taking up Canadian residence, you should ensure that you and your professional tax advisor have discussed the implications of the types of income you may be receiving both prior to and after entering Canada, as well as the timing of the receipt of various types of income. In particular, you should review any foreign incentive compensation that might be payable to you. Depending on the circumstances, you might want to arrange to receive income such as bonuses, stock options and payments from profit sharing plans prior to entering Canada.

If you will be selling your foreign residence and acquiring a Canadian one, it is probably more beneficial for you to sell the former before taking up Canadian residence. If you intend to rent out your foreign home, you will be subject to tax in Canada on the net rental income. If you will also be subject to tax on rental income in your "home" country, you should evaluate the benefits of renting out your home versus leaving it vacant or even disposing of it.

You should also consider the timing of your arrival in Canada. The best date will depend on your tax liabilities in both the country you are leaving and in Canada. Your professional advisor can help you make a detailed estimate.

Taxable Canadian property

Taxable Canadian property includes, among other things, real property (land and buildings, for example), capital property used in carrying on business in Canada, shares of a private corporation that is resident or deemed to be resident in Canada, and shares of a public corporation if at any time during the five years immediately preceding the disposition, the non-resident and persons with whom he or she did not deal at arm's length owned 25% or more of the issued shares of any class of its capital stock.

Unlike other capital property, you are not deemed to have disposed of taxable Canadian property when you give up your Canadian residence because when you do ultimately dispose of it you are required to file a Canadian income tax return and pay tax on any resulting capital gains.

You may elect to deem other capital property to be taxable Canadian property. If you make this election, you must provide Revenue Canada with acceptable security equal to the amount of tax that would have been payable on the deemed disposition of the property had you not made the election.

Making this election could improve your cash flow. If the deemed disposition rules apply, you have to pay any tax on a resulting capital gain even though you have not actually disposed of anything and have not received any proceeds. If you make the election (and can post sufficient security) you will not have to come up with the cash immediately.

If you make the election, you should exclude enough capital property to allow you to deduct the unused portion of your capital gains deduction. Keep in mind that any further increase in the value of the property you have elected to be treated as taxable Canadian property will be subject to Canadian tax when you actually dispose of it.

This election has pitfalls, so you should discuss it with your advisor before proceeding.

⚜ Québec

If you are resident in Québec, the comments above generally apply to Québec taxes. However, the following exceptions should be noted:

• Gain sharing receipts

Starting in 1993, amounts received by an eligible employee under a qualifying gain sharing plan may be deducted in the calculation of Québec taxable income to a maximum of $3,000 per year. A cumulative maximum of $6,000 applies for the five-year period starting in the year of registration of the first plan in which the employee participates.

Québec Sales Tax

• Introduction of a single sales tax rate

— The rate applicable to properties (as of May 13, 1994) was reduced from 8% to 6.5%. The rate for services and immovables was raised from 4% to 6.5%.

— The 5% and 9% rates on insurance premiums remain unchanged.

• Purchase of a new home

— A rebate equal to 36% of the QST paid on the purchase of a new home costing $175,000 or less will be available. A decreasing rebate will also be granted on a house costing between $175,000 and $200,000.

• Sales of used road vehicles

— The price of used road vehicles on which the QST will apply as of June 1, 1994, will be the higher of the consideration paid by the purchaser and the value of the vehicle given in the Canadian Red Book less $500.

New refundable child tax credit

• The tax deduction for child care expenses will be replaced by a refundable tax credit equal to a percentage of the amount paid during the year for child care, up to a maximum of $5,000. The rate of tax credit will be based on net family income, as indicated in the table below.

	From	To	Tax credit as a % of eligible expenses
Net family income	$0	$10,000	From 75% to 44%
	$10,000	$34,000	40%
	$34,000	$48,000	From 39% to 27%
	$48,000		26.4%

The amount of expenses eligible for the tax credit for the year will be determined by the rules used for the child care expense deduction. The refundable tax credit may be claimed by either spouse.

Increase in taxable benefits

In its May 20, 1993 budget, Québec proposed to treat as taxable benefits the premiums paid by an employer under a group term life insurance policy, in relation to the first $25,000 of coverage, and those paid under an accident insurance or private health insurance plan. The federal government harmonized its tax rule with this measure for benefits granted after the month of June 1994. The value of any benefits received under some insurance plans may be adjusted by the Québec tax authorities when taxpayers receive a releve 22 form from the plans' administrators.

• Automobile expenses – taxable benefits

The Ministère du Revenu is expected to harmonize its rules with the announcement made by the federal Department of Finance regarding a reduction, from 12 cents per kilometre to 9 cents per kilometre, of the fixed rate applicable to the determination of the taxable benefit for the personal use of an automobile provided by an employer to an employee who is mainly engaged in the sale or lease of automobiles. This reduced rate would apply to the 1994 and subsequent taxation years.

• Tuition fees

The amount of tuition fees is used as the basis for the determination of the nonrefundable tax credit described on page XX. In Québec, tuition fees are deductible only by the student, and cannot be transferred to the student's father or mother. However, a person upon whom the student is dependent may increase his or her dependent child credit if the student is registered full-time in a post-secondary institution. The person requesting the credit must file form TP-697 with his or her Québec income tax return.

Health services fund contribution

Until recently, only employers paid a health services tax based on employment earnings of their employees. The 1993 budget extended the health services tax to other types of income earned by individuals. The tax is paid by individuals resident in Québec on December 31 as part of their overall income tax bill.

The health services tax will be payable on notional "total income", including net business income, investment income, pension or retirement income and taxable capital gains. Excluded from the calculation will be those items already subject to the employer health tax (i.e., wages) and the gross-up on dividends from Canadian corporations. In addition, the 1994 budget indicates that taxpayers will no longer be subject to the Health Services Fund contribution on amounts received as Old Age Security benefits, beginning with the 1994 taxation year.

Certain deductions will be permitted in arriving at "total income", including amounts subject to the federal clawback, expenditures incurred to earn investment income, and a general exemption of $5,000.

This new contribution will be eligible for a non-refundable tax credit of 20% in the individual income tax return.

Temporary assignments in Québec

If you are a non-resident of Canada and you were employed in Québec at any time in the year or in a previous year, you will generally be subject to Québec tax on your employment income and will be required to file a Québec income tax return.

Temporary assignments outside Canada

If you are a Canadian, resided in Québec during 1994, and have been or will be employed abroad for 30 consecutive days or more beginning

54 in the year or the preceding year, you may be allowed a deduction in computing net income equal to all or part of the employment income earned abroad. A full deduction is available if you are abroad for 12 periods of 30 consecutive days or more. This deduction is available for the same types of employers and activities as those mentioned in this chapter for the federal overseas employment tax credit (see page 46). In addition, the following activities are eligible for this deduction:

• the setting up of an automated office system, data processing system or telephone data system or similar system, if that activity is the principal purpose of the contract;

• scientific or technical services; and

• management or administration related to an activity covered by the deduction for workers outside Québec.

Beginning in 1995, the deduction will be granted in the determination of taxable (rather than net) income.

Taxable Québec property

Québec has rules similar to those applicable to taxable Canadian property, but they apply only to property situated in Québec that is referred to as "taxable Québec property".

An exception to the general rule is that Québec will remit income tax of an individual non-resident of Canada, not doing business in Canada, realizing a capital gain on sale of share of a corporation resident in Québec other than a public corporation. The taxpayer will, however, pay the 52% federal non-resident surtax on basic federal tax.

Deceased persons

• Deadline for filing the 1994 income tax return

The income tax return of a person deceased in 1994 must be filed by the later of:

- May 1, 1995; and
- Six months following the date of the person's death.

The 1994 income tax return of a person who dies during the first four months of 1995 must be filed within six months of the person's death.

• Duties on land transfer arising after a death

When land is transferred upon a person's death, an heir who does not reside in Canada will no longer be required to pay duties on the transfer of the land. This change applies to any land transferred as part of a succession opened after May 12, 1994.

Immovable transfer duties

• Transfer between common-law spouses

The Act respecting Duties on Transfers of Immovables (DTI) will be amended to give common-law spouses the same privileges as those afforded to married spouses respecting the exemption for transfers between spouses. A definition of the word "spouse" identical to that in the *Taxation Act* will be incorporated into the DTI and will apply to any transfer of immovables occurring after May 12, 1994.

• Transfers between related natural persons carried out through a trust

The DTI will be amended to exempt transfers involving a trust and its beneficiary if the beneficiary is a natural person related to the person who originally transferred the property to the trust in keeping with a parental or matrimonial relationship that would otherwise be exempt under the DTI. This amendment will apply to the transfer of any immovable to a beneficiary from a trust after May 12, 1994.

• Exemption for transfers between natural persons related in the ascending line

It is possible for the transfer of an immovable involving persons who are not related for the purposes of the exemptions granted to be carried out without the payment of duties, where the transaction is structured so as to first transfer the immovables to a common ascendant.

An amendment will be made to the DTI to prevent the descending line exemption from being granted if the transferor himself has acquired the immovable from a person related to him in the descending line (therefore, after the initial transfer) or from a trust that had acquired the property from a person to whom the transferor was related in the descending line at the time of acquisition, and did not retain ownership of the immovable for at least two years. This amendment will apply after May 12, 1994.

Québec tax incentives

• Tax holiday for employees of an international financial centre (IFC)

A two-year tax holiday may be granted to foreign employees of an IFC specializing in the field of international financial transactions. In addition, following this two-year period, under certain conditions, those employees may be eligible for an income tax exemption on allowances paid to them, up to a maximum of 50% of their basic eligible salary.

Beginning in 1995, the IFC deduction will reduce the taxpayer's taxable income, rather than net income.

• Extension of the tax holiday granted to foreign researchers

To further encourage researchers specializing in R&D to come to Québec, the measure granting a two-year tax holiday to foreign researchers has been renewed, under the same terms as those provided under current tax legislation, for an additional period of three years. Thus, a two-year tax holiday may be granted to a foreign researcher whose employment contract is signed prior to January 1, 1997 and whose salary constitutes, for the employer, an R&D expenditure made in Québec no later than December 31, 1998.

Other Québec Exceptions

As of July 1, 1992, Québec modified its sales tax system (QST). With these changes, the QST, much like the federal GST, requires that a separate QST component be added to determine the total amount of a taxable benefit, in most cases.

With respect to stock options, Québec's taxation system is harmonized with the federal system for stock options exercised after May 2, 1991. For options exercised earlier, unlike the federal rules, the liability to pay tax arises only in the year in which you dispose of the shares, if they are acquired through a qualified stock option plan.

In Québec, receipts for moving expenses must be filed with the tax return.

Since 1993, in the case of salaried employees paid on commission, expenses – which may not be deducted in excess of any commissions paid – must be reduced by an amount not exceeding the lesser of $750 and 6% of total compensation (salary plus commissions).

In its 1994 budget, Québec announced that it would not harmonize its tax credit for the elderly with that of the federal tax system.

Following the Québec budget of May 12, 1994, amendments will be made to the *Taxation Act* to give an individual – other than a trust – the choice of excluding from his or her income, in the year in which he or she receives it, a retroactive payment of at least $300. Retroactive payments include employment income received as the result of a judgement or an agreement between parties in judicial proceedings or alimony arrears. This choice will enable individuals to pay any tax related to retroactive payment as if they had received the payment in the years to which it applied. This measure is applicable to amounts received after December 31, 1993.

Québec generally follows the terms of the tax treaties signed by Canada regarding what is excluded from income. The only separate tax treaty that Québec has entered into is with France.

Owners/Managers

Owners/Managers

Although "owner/manager" is not a term found in the Income Tax Act, it is a convenient way of referring to anybody who owns and runs a business. This chapter deals first with unincorporated businesses, and then with private companies.

Unincorporated businesses

Carrying on business

The distinction between income from a business and income from employment or from investments is important. If you are indeed in business, you will be able to deduct reasonable business expenses not deductible by an employee or an investor.

For tax purposes, a business includes a profession, calling, trade, manufacture, and just about anything else that could possibly be considered a business. Being employed or holding an office, however, is not a business.

If you are self-employed, i.e., you are not an employee and you have not formed a corporation through which you will provide your services, then you must determine whether you are in business. This will not generally pose a problem if you are earning your living from the activity. Generally, you must have a reasonable expectation of profit from the activity for it to be considered a business, and you must pursue the activity in a manner likely to bring you a profit. While you need not produce a profit immediately, or even have a history of making profits, you must have a reasonable chance of doing so.

An individual can have more than one business, in which case the profits of each must be calculated separately.

If you carry on an unincorporated business, you may be able to make an election to recognize capital gains accrued to February 22, 1994 on capital property.

Employed versus self-employed

Whether you are employed or self-employed is not always easy to determine. The answer will depend on your particular circumstances, and often boils down to how much control the person paying for your services exercises over your work. For example, if the payor controls your work hours, requires you to work on his premises and furnishes you with all the equipment, supplies and office help that you need, you likely would still be considered an employee in the eyes of Revenue Canada. If you provide services to a number of different parties and you determine the nature and degree of service and are in a position to prioritize their demands, you are likely self-employed. Other tests include whether you provide your own tools, whether you have an opportunity for profit, and whether you have a risk of loss.

Partnerships

An unincorporated business can be carried on as a proprietorship or a partnership. Each partner is taxed on his or her share of the partnership income in essentially the same way as a proprietor. Based on a predetermined formula, the partnership computes the income that is allocated to each partner. A partner reports the allocated share and deducts expenses incurred personally, such as interest and automobile expenses, to determine his or her net income from the business.

Tax Tip

A husband and wife, or other family members, can carry on a business through a partnership. It is generally advisable to have a written partnership agreement to support the profit-sharing formula and the basis of contributions to the business in the event that Revenue Canada raises questions.

Tax Tip

Partnerships with more than five partners are required to file annual financial information. The partnership provides reporting slips to partners for inclusion in their own returns.

Professionals

Professionals may carry on business as sole proprietors, partners, or, depending on the legislation and the rules of the professional bodies, through corporations. Designated professionals (accountants, chiropractors, dentists, lawyers, medical doctors and veterinarians) are permitted to elect to exclude the value of work in progress from income. If they do not make the election, they follow the normal accrual rules and report income as it is earned, rather than as payment is received.

Instalments

A self-employed individual earning business or professional income must pay tax directly to Revenue Canada. Quarterly instalments of tax are due on:

- March 15;

- June 15;

- September 15; and

- December 15.

The prescribed rate of interest charged during a calendar quarter on late or deficient payments of tax is set each quarter:

		Prescribed rate*	
		Other than Québec	Québec
Quarter of 1994	1st	7%	8% or 5%**
	2nd	6%	7% or 5%**
	3rd	8%	9% or 5.5%**
	4th	9%	10% or 5.5%**

* The rate for deemed interest on employee and shareholder loans is lower than the rates shown (see page 13).

** The Québec government pays the lower rate on amounts it owes to taxpayers.

Additional penalties may also be imposed on late or deficient tax instalments where interest in excess of $1,000 is owing.

Choice of year end

Tax Tip

Careful selection of a year end for your business could result in deferral of tax. The benefits of deferral do carry an ultimate price to be paid when the business ends or is sold. The deferred tax liabilities will become due after the income has been earned. The prudent owner/manager will have put away a sufficient portion of those profits to meet the deferred tax liability. Professional advice is strongly recommended.

You may choose to have your fiscal year end at any time in the year. The fiscal year of your business cannot exceed 12 months; your first fiscal year may, however, be shorter than normal. Once you have selected your fiscal year end, you must obtain written approval from Revenue Canada to have it changed. The change must have underlying business reasons.

Tax Tip

Although changes have been made to the basis for determining who is required to make quarterly income tax instalments (see page 190), instalments may be delayed for as much as two years by selecting an appropriate year end for your business. Remember that you will have to include in your personal income tax return for a particular calendar year income from the fiscal year of your business that ends in that calendar year. Discuss your instalment requirements with your tax advisor. Under–estimating your instalments may be costly.

Automobiles

The rules for self–employed individuals are not nearly as complex as those for employees who are supplied with a car by their employers. The restrictions on capital cost allowance claims, monthly interest charges and monthly lease payments that apply to employees claiming automobile expenses, however, apply equally to the self–employed. To make the most of automobile expense claims, you should keep records of expenses incurred as well as details of personal and business kilometres driven.

Tax Tip

You do not have to file supporting vouchers or documents with your income tax return but you should keep them in case they are requested by Revenue Canada. They may turn out to be crucial if you are challenged.

If you use a car partly for business and partly for personal purposes, the deductible amount of car expenses is:

$$[\text{operating expenses} + \text{fixed expenses}]$$
$$\text{X}$$
$$\left[\frac{\text{distance driven to earn business income}}{\text{total distance driven}} \right]$$

Expenses incurred in travelling between different premises of the same business are deductible. Expenses incurred in travelling from your home are not deductible, unless you can establish that your home is the base of your business operations. If you have an office or other fixed place of business located elsewhere, your home will not be regarded as the base of your business operations.

The fact that you render all your services at some other persons' place of business will not necessarily make that place your base, and you may still be able to deduct costs of travelling there from your base at home.

If you are a GST registrant, you may be eligible to claim input tax credits for a portion of the GST you paid on reasonable car expenses.

If you are paying automobile allowances to employees, you may deduct those allowances only to the extent that they do not exceed the limits in the table below. If you choose to pay your employees more than the allowable amounts, you cannot deduct the excess unless the full amount of the allowances is taxable in the employees' hands. If this is the case, you should ensure that your employees keep records of the distance they drive and provide you with their records so that you can support your claims. The employees will be able to deduct their business-related expenses and may be better off than they would have been with a nontaxable receipt.

If you are a GST registrant, you may be able to claim a notional input tax credit (7/107 of the allowance paid) to the extent the allowance is both reasonable (i.e., not taxable to the employee) and deductible to you.

		Maximum deductible automobile allowance (per kilometre)	
		All provinces	Both territories
Business driving in the year	First 5,000 kilometres	$0.31	$0.35
	Beyond 5,000 kilometres	$0.25	$0.29

66 | Depreciable assets

While everyday business expenses can be deducted from business income, the cost of capital assets is deductible over a longer period. This is accomplished through the capital cost allowance (CCA) rules, which provide varying rates of write-off, depending on the type of assets involved.

For example, office equipment and furniture are depreciated at a rate of 20% per annum; the rate for general purpose computers and systems software and for automobiles is 30%; and the rate for a building acquired after 1987 is usually 4%. All are calculated on a declining-balance basis.

Generally, in the year in which you buy an asset, CCA is limited to one-half of the rate to which you would ordinarily be entitled. In addition, if your fiscal period is less than a year, you will be required to prorate the CCA amount otherwise determined.

Since CCA is based on the undepreciated capital cost of assets at the end of the year, you will not be able to claim CCA in the year in which you dispose of a business asset unless you continue to own other similar assets that are pooled for CCA purposes with the asset that you sold. On the other hand, you may be entitled to a terminal loss if there is a balance in the class at the end of the year, but no assets.

The CCA rules were recently amended to permit a taxpayer to elect to place eligible property in a separate class for CCA purposes. Eligible property includes general-purpose electronic data processing equipment, photocopiers and certain electronic communications equipment such as facsimile transmission devices and telephone and related ancillary equipment, where the cost is $1,000 or more.

A separate class election does not change the specified CCA rate on the equipment. Rather, it allows a taxpayer to calculate a separate CCA deduction on one or more particular pieces of equipment. The separate class election ensures that, on the disposition of all the property in the class, any remaining undepreciated cost of the equipment may be fully deductible as a terminal loss. The election will benefit taxpayers who acquire eligible equipment that depreciates faster than is implicit in the CCA rate for property of that class.

The measure is effective for property acquired after April 26, 1993. The election must be made in the income tax return for the taxation year in which the property is acquired.

Tax Tip

Timing is an important consideration when you are purchasing and selling capital assets. Try to purchase assets before the end of your fiscal year so that you are at least entitled to claim one-half of the normal CCA. When disposing of an asset, try to time the sale after year end so that the full CCA claim is made in the previous year. Generally, you must take delivery of an asset and put it into use in order to claim CCA in the first year.

Office in the home

If you operate an office in your home, you can claim supplies and other expenses that are entirely associated with the business, such as a business phone. Expenses that are shared with the operation of the home, such as utilities, insurance, property taxes, rent and mortgage interest are generally apportioned according to the space used. Depreciation on your home is also deductible, but this will reduce your claim for the principal residence exemption on the sale of your home. Normally, claiming depreciation expense on your home offers little or no advantage. The table on page 68 outlines these considerations.

If your work space is used exclusively to earn business income and for regularly and continually meeting your clients, customers or patients, the space set aside for your business must be a room or rooms used exclusively for the business. Setting up a computer and filing cabinets at one end of the living room will not entitle you to claim home office expenses.

68 | Home office expenses – self-employed

Should be deducted (if conditions are satisfied*)	Should generally not be deducted
Most expenses are deductible, including property taxes and mortgage interest attributable to the office. Maintenance expenses include: – fuel – light bulbs – electricity – minor repairs – cleaning materials	Capital cost allowance (due to the principal residence exemption)

* Expenses are deductible only if the workplace is:
• your principal place of business; **or**
• used by you both:
  – exclusively for the purpose of earning business income; **and**
  – "on a regular and continuous basis" for meeting clients or patients.

If you operate a full-time business out of your home, you will be able to deduct eligible expenses that relate to the work space. If you operate a part-time business, or have other office space out of which you conduct your business, you may be denied a deduction for office in the home expenses.

Tax Tip

Home office expenses may be deducted only from income earned from the business carried on in the home, i.e., they may not be deducted from other sources of income. You may, however, carry excess expenses forward to a future year and deduct them from income generated by the business.

Business meals and entertainment expenses

Until recently, 80% of business meals and entertainment expenses was deductible for tax purposes; the other 20% was borne by the business. The 1994 federal budget proposes to further limit the deductible portion to 50%. The new limit applies to expenses for meals, beverages and entertainment consumed or enjoyed after February 1994.

A similar restriction applies for purposes of the GST. Accordingly, only 50% of the GST paid on business meals and entertainment expenses may be recovered as an input tax credit.

Tax Tip

The proposed 50% limitation does not apply to incidental beverages and refreshments (coffee and doughnuts, for example) provided to clients visiting your office, or at conferences, seminars or conventions.

Tax Tip

Meal and entertainment expenses specifically identified on your invoice and billed directly back to your clients are not subject to the proposed 50% limitation.

Retirement plans

If you have an unincorporated business, contributions to an RRSP may be the only avenue available to you to accumulate retirement savings. Your net income from the business, i.e., business income after expenses, is considered to be earned income for the purposes of determining the maximum amount that you may contribute to your RRSP.

If you incorporate your business (see below), you could establish an IPP for yourself (see page 30). As discussed below, the decision to incorporate is complicated, and the opportunity to establish an IPP is only one factor that should be considered.

Salaries to spouse and children

If your spouse or children work in the business, salaries paid to them will be deductible for tax purposes as long as the wages are reasonable in relation to the work performed. Of course, the wages received will be taxable in their hands.

Tax Tip

Salaries paid to your spouse or children will enable them to make their own RRSP contributions and to contribute to the Canada or Québec Pension Plans.

Private companies

Setting up the corporation

Unlike a sole proprietorship or a partnership, a corporation is a separate legal entity, an artificial person required to file a tax return and pay taxes quite separate from its owners. You may transfer your business assets to a corporation, generally without tax consequences to you, subject to certain restrictions. In addition to holding shares of the corporation (equity), you may also hold debt.

Tax Tip

You will incur expenses in establishing and maintaining a corporation that you would not have with an unincorporated business. You should evaluate carefully both the timing and consequences of incorporating to see if the benefits outweigh the costs.

Tax deferral

The income from an unincorporated business is included in your personal income tax return and, therefore, taxed at your personal marginal tax rate. In contrast, if you incorporate your business, its income belongs to the corporation, and will be taxed at corporate rates. Your personal income tax return will be affected only to the extent that the corporation distributes its earnings to you as salary, dividends, or interest.

The rate of corporate tax will depend on the type of income the corporation is earning as well as on the province(s) in which it carries on business. For example, up to $200,000 of active business income may be taxed at a combined federal and provincial rate as low as 18% (even lower if a provincial tax holiday applies). The top marginal rate for an individual earning the same type of income directly would be about triple the corporate rate.

The 1994 federal budget proposes to eliminate the preferential tax rate for very large private corporations. The $200,000 business limit will be reduced on a straight line basis for Canadian-controlled private corporations (CCPCs) with taxable capital employed in Canada of between $10 and $15 million in the preceding year. This will eliminate the benefit of the small business deduction for those CCPCs with taxable capital of $15 million or more. The measure will apply to taxation years ending after June 30, 1994.

If you incorporate your business and retain earnings in the corporation for growth, you will be able to defer tax to the extent that the earnings are not distributed to you.

Integration

If you are the sole shareholder of a corporation, you and the corporation constitute two separate tax-paying entities. Salary that the corporation pays you is an expense that reduces the income of the corporation. For you, it is income.

The corporation will pay tax on its taxable income; income that is distributed to you from the corporation by way of dividends will be subject to a second tier of tax through the personal tax system. The concept of integration mitigates the effects of this potential double incidence of tax.

According to the integration concept, income earned through a corporation and distributed to an individual shareholder should attract the same amount of tax as if that individual had earned the income directly. In practice, however, integration would work perfectly only if the combined federal and provincial rate of tax is 20% for a corporation and 43.5% for an individual, and if there are no surtaxes.

Because actual corporate and personal tax rates differ from the rates necessary to achieve perfect integration, your total taxes will vary depending on whether income comes directly to you or through a corporation. The differences will depend on the type of income, your province of residence, and the jurisdiction in which the corporation carries on business.

Whether earning income directly or through a corporation is preferable will depend on your personal circumstances. Active business income earned by a corporation, taxed at the small business rate and distributed as a dividend will usually attract less total tax than if you earned the income directly. On the other hand, income taxed at the top corporate rate and subsequently distributed to a shareholder in the top personal tax rate band will suffer double taxation.

Tax Tip

Incorporating your business involves making decisions that are both emotional and practical. Complex issues must be addressed, and the choices you make can be costly to undo. Ensure that your professional tax advisor is involved every step of the way.

$500,000 (or $400,000) enhanced capital gains exemption

Tax Tip

When you start a business, keep the business assets in a corporation separate from one that holds investment or non-business assets.

Shares of Qualifying Small Business Corporations may be eligible for an enhanced capital gains exemption of $400,000 ($500,000 if you haven't used the $100,000 capital gains exemption. Refer to page 98 for further details.) A small business corporation (SBC) is generally defined as a Canadian-controlled private corporation (CCPC) of which all or substantially all the assets (more than 90% according to Revenue Canada) are used in an active business carried on primarily in Canada. The corporation must be an SBC when the shares are disposed of and the shares must not have been held by anyone other than the taxpayer or related persons throughout the immediately preceding 24 months. In addition, throughout the same period, more than 50% of the fair market value of the assets of the corporation must be used in an active business it carries on primarily in Canada.

Tax Tip

Removing any non-qualifying assets from your corporation now will help you meet the "all or substantially all" test in the definition of an SBC when the shares are eventually sold or transferred.

Tax Tip

If the shares in your small business corporation have substantial accrued capital gains, consider electing to sell some of the shares to your spouse at fair market value, triggering a capital gain, up to $400,000 of which could be exempt. Professional tax advice is a must because of alternative minimum tax (AMT) and other considerations.

Election for Private Corporations Going Public

While shares of a public corporation do not qualify as small business corporation shares, individuals may benefit from the enhanced capital gains exemption when a small business corporation is about to go public. An individual may elect to be treated as having disposed of all of the shares of a class of the capital stock of the small business corporation immediately before it becomes a public corporation. The individual will have to specify an amount to be the deemed proceeds of disposition. The proceeds may be the adjusted cost base of the shares or any higher amount up to their fair market value. The individual will be treated as having reacquired the shares immediately after the elected disposition at a cost equal to the specified proceeds. These new provisions will enable an individual to claim the enhanced capital gains exemption in respect of the disposition of the qualifying shares.

Salary versus dividends

One of the major decisions for an owner-managed corporation is the split between salary and dividends. Your personal tax position as owner/manager, as well as that of the corporation itself, must be taken into account in determining the optimum compensation package.

Rules of thumb help determine the best amount to be paid as salary to owners and the amount to be taxed in the corporation and subsequently distributed as dividends. The rules of thumb assume that all amounts paid are reasonable in the circumstances, do not take cash requirements for living expenses into account, and do not consider a possible sale of the business and the capital gains exemption discussed below.

Tax Tip

Using salary or bonuses to reduce the active business income of the corporation to $200,000 annually will generally be advantageous to the owner-managed corporation.

The payment of salary, rather than dividends, should be considered whenever the combined federal and provincial tax rate of the corporation exceeds 20%. This will generally hold true where the corporation is earning business income that is not eligible for the small business deduction.

Tax Tip

The accrual of a bonus may be preferable to the payment of salary. A bonus paid within 180 days of a corporate year end will be deductible to the corporation; personal tax will be withheld when the bonus is paid.

Tax Tip

Consider paying yourself sufficient salary to enable you to make maximum Canada or Québec Pension Plan contributions, as well as to contribute the maximum to your RRSP. The contribution limit for your RRSP is based on 18% of your earned income in the previous year. The maximum you can contribute to your RRSP in 1994 is $13,500, which means that you must have earned income of $75,000 in 1993 in order to make the maximum contribution to your RRSP in 1994. (You will need earned income of $80,556 in 1994 to make the maximum RRSP contribution in 1995, which is $14,500.)

See page 26 for details on RRSP contribution limits.

Directors' fees

In addition to the role you perform in your own company, you may also be a director, either of another corporation or of your own. If you are a director and are earning directors' fees, those fees are considered to be employment income and must be included on your tax return. Directors' fees are earned income for the purposes of determining how much you can contribute to your or a spousal RRSP. Refer to page 189 as well for a discussion concerning directors' liability.

| ## Salaries to spouse and children

A corporation may provide an opportunity for income splitting with your spouse or children. Salaries may be paid to family members as long as services are actually performed and the amount of salaries and wages is reasonable. Generally, salaries would be considered to be reasonable if they are representative of an amount that would have to be paid to an arm's length party for similar services.

Paying reasonable wages to family members for actual services rendered has four advantages:

(a) the salaries will be deductible to the corporation;

(b) the salaries will be taxed in the hands of the recipients, and depending on the circumstances, probably at rates lower than the top marginal rate;

(c) the salaries will enable family members to contribute to their own RRSPs; and

(d) the tuition fee and education tax credits may mean that salaries paid to children attending university may attract little or no tax at all.

Planning around your CNIL

A corporation may provide you with some flexibility in arranging your personal concerns. If you will realize capital gains in the year from the disposition of Qualified Small Business Corporation shares that will not be sheltered from tax by the enhanced capital gains exemption because you have cumulative net investment losses (CNILs), consider arranging to receive sufficient interest or dividend income from the corporation to eliminate your CNIL.

This strategy may fully or partially restore your access to the enhanced capital gains exemption (see page 101 for more about CNILs).

Tax Tip

Curing a CNIL problem in this fashion will be particularly important if you will be making an election in your 1994 return with respect to capital gains realized or accrued on other capital property (see page 93 for further details).

Québec

If you are an owner/manager residing in Québec, the following differences in the Québec legislation should be noted:

Depreciable assets

Québec has a 100% CCA deduction for:

• computers;

• systems software; and

• machinery and equipment,

used for manufacturing and processing in Québec, without the half-year rule applying, if they are acquired after May 12, 1988.

The same tax treatment is granted for intangible property acquired after May 16, 1989, such as patents, licences, permits (but not trademarks and industrial drawings), knowledge, know-how, techniques, processes or formulae, whether protected or not, acquired in order to implement an innovation or an invention.

Owner/Managers

The 1993 Québec budget proposed to harmonize the Québec tax regulations with the new federal provisions that allow separate CCA classes for certain goods (see page 66).

78 Entertainment expenses

In its May 20, 1993 budget, Québec announced the reduction of the deductible portion for entertainment expenses from 80% to 50%, for expenditures made after the day of the budget speech.

Instalments

The Québec prescribed rate of interest charged on late or deficient instalments of tax for the third quarter of 1994 is 9%. An additional interest at the rate of 10% per annum is payable on any late or deficient instalment that is less than 90% of the required instalment.

Health services fund contribution

For more information about this new contribution, please refer to page 54.

Recent changes

- The interest-free period for payment of an assessment has been extended from 30 to 45 days, after which additional interest will be payable by the taxpayer. This measure applies to notices of assessment mailed after June 30, 1994.

- The presumed date of payment to the Ministère du Revenu, when payment is made directly to a financial institution, will no longer be the date stamped by a public employee of the Ministère du Revenu on the payment slip, but rather the date on which payment is received by the financial institution. This measure will apply as of July 1, 1994.

Québec's new Civil Code

Québec's new Civil Code came into effect January 1, 1994. See your legal advisor.

Annual information forms

Québec requires that partnerships file annual financial information forms that are different from federal forms.

Investors

Investors

You are an investor even if you do not have an extensive portfolio. If you own your home or maintain a bank account you should review this chapter.

Astute investors never lose sight of the fact that it is the after-tax result of their activities that matters, not the nominal yield on their investments. Tax is only one element in the complex process of making investment decisions. The investment's yield and risk should always be considered ahead of income tax aspects. While tax itself seldom motivates a particular transaction, it can be a crucial factor when deciding among alternative investments with similar pre-tax yields.

Financial rewards from investment fall into two broad categories for tax purposes: investment income and capital gains. This chapter covers both, along with tax shelters (investments with a significant tax reduction component).

Investment income

Interest and dividends

Interest and dividends are taxed differently. All interest income you received and generally all interest income that accrued to you during the year is fully taxable in your hands. Even a small amount of interest on your savings account for which you did not receive a T5 slip from the bank is taxable.

Dividends from taxable Canadian corporations are included in your income along with a 25% "gross-up" of the amount you received. You can claim a federal dividend tax credit of 16⅔% of the actual dividend (equivalent to 13⅓% of the grossed-up amount) in arriving at your basic federal tax. You may claim the dividend tax credit only in the year the dividend was received.

Because provincial taxes are generally a little more than half of basic federal tax, the value of the dividend tax credit increases to about 26% of the dividend. On the other hand, the combined federal and provincial tax payable on the gross-up adds about 11% tax, at top marginal rates. Once the federal surtax is accounted for, the net effect is a reduction in tax of about 15 percentage points. (This reduction is not as great as it used to be, however.)

The bar charts compare the income tax on $1,000 of dividends under the gross-up/credit arrangement and under ordinary rules

How the gross up and dividend tax credit reduce taxes at top marginal rates

Without gross-up and dividend tax credit

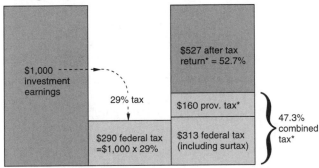

With gross-up and dividend tax credit

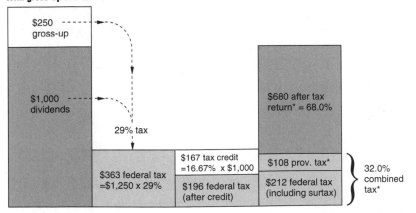

* Provincial tax, and therefore the after-tax return, will vary depending on actual provincial tax rates. This example assumes provincial taxes are 55% of federal taxes (before the federal surtax).

84   (i.e., as if no gross-up or credit applied) for a taxpayer at the top
rate. The 32.0% combined tax that results from the gross-up and
dividend tax credit is about 15 percentage points less than the 47.3%
calculated without them.

This approximate 15 percentage point effective reduction in the
tax on Canadian dividends means that in 1994, an individual in the
top marginal tax bracket would require a gross yield of only about
6% on a dividend to generate the same net after-tax yield as an
investment earning 8% interest (see Appendix 3).

Annual accrual rules

Generally, all interest that accrued in the year on investments you
acquired after 1989 must be included in your income for tax purposes, even if you did not actually receive the income. The types of
investments to which this rule applies include compound interest
debt obligations, deferred annuities and certain life insurance policies. The amount to be reported is the interest earned or accrued
during each complete investment year.

For example, if you made a long-term investment on September 1,
1993, the first year's interest must be calculated to the end of August
1994. This amount, whether you receive a T5 slip or not, must be
reported on your 1994 income tax return. Similarly, interest accrued
on that investment from September 1, 1994 to August 31, 1995 will
have to be reported on your 1995 return.

An investment will be treated as having been acquired after 1989
if, after that year, it has been materially altered, for example, by
extending its term. Of course, these rules do not apply to interest
earned in a statutory deferred income plan such as your RRSP.

Prior to 1990, you had the choice of reporting accrued interest
income from these types of securities annually, or deferring tax for
up to three years by reporting accrued income every third calendar
year after the year of purchase. Accordingly, if you purchased a debt

obligation before 1990 (but after November 12, 1981, when the rules changed) and assuming there has been no material change in the terms of the security, you may continue to report accrued interest using the method you have in the past: annually or in the third calendar year after purchase and every three years thereafter.

Tax Tip

If you currently hold certain "locked-in" compound interest securities that were acquired before November 13, 1981, you may want to hold on to them. This type of security is not subject to the accrual rules, i.e., you don't have to pay tax on the earnings until the contract matures and you actually receive the interest.

Debt obligations that are held in connection with a U.S. Individual Retirement Account (IRA) are excluded from the accrual rules.

Tax Tip

Bonds and other debt instruments that mature should be cashed and reinvested promptly, because they pay no interest after the maturity date. Canada Savings Bonds should be reviewed every October.

Life insurance policies

Life insurance could be an important part of your personal financial planning.

Traditionally, life insurance has often been used as an investment vehicle as well as a means of providing funds to an insured's estate or beneficiaries on the insured's death. Nevertheless, many people opted for "pure" or "term" life insurance policies, which simply paid a stipulated amount on the insured's death, but had no investment component. This preference often reflected the expectation of low investment returns or at least uncertainty about the return available on non-term policies. In recent years, however, the investment aspect has taken on new importance and has become more attractive. One of the major reasons for this is the favourable tax treatment provided for "exempt" policies. Any investment income earned in an exempt policy is exempt from tax. Furthermore, any amounts paid out under an exempt policy on the death of the insured are also exempt from tax. In a sense, the investment element of an exempt policy is a perfect tax shelter, in that the investment income can be earned and paid out without ever having been subject to tax.

To be "exempt", a policy must satisfy certain complex rules covering the relationship between the "pure" insurance portion of the policy and the investment portion.

In effect, these rules require that a certain portion of your premium be used by the insurance company to provide pure insurance coverage, rather than being invested on your behalf. Whether a policy meets these requirements is essentially under the control of the insurance company. Any income accruing on the savings component of a non-exempt policy would be subject to the annual accrual rules referred to in the preceding section.

The other development that has made life insurance more attractive as an investment is that insurance companies have become more willing to disclose mortality and administrative costs, and even to guarantee minimum interest rates. This makes insurance policies easier to understand and makes their investment merits easier to assess.

The tax shelter aspect of an exempt policy has several potential uses, particularly after other tax shelter opportunities (e.g., RRSP contributions) have been exhausted. For example, a life insurance policy could be used:

- to fund supplementary retirement benefits;

- to fund a "retirement compensation arrangement". (This is an arrangement formally provided for under the *Income Tax Act* for an employer to set aside funds for the retirement of employees. The investment income earned on those funds is normally subject to tax.);

- as a vehicle for making charitable contributions. (A donation tax credit is available for the value of a policy assigned to a charity or for premiums paid on a policy on your life owned by a charity.); or

- in connection with corporate buy-sell arrangements. (If you have a private corporation that owns a policy on your life and pays the premiums, any proceeds received by the corporation increases its capital dividend account (CDA). The balance in a corporation's CDA can be paid out as a tax-free dividend to the corporation's shareholders).

You may also be able to get at the tax-sheltered earnings through taxable draws on the cash surrender value of the policy or by pledging the policy as collateral for a loan.

Another advantage that may be available is protection of your assets. The investment portion of an exempt policy may be excluded by law from the reach of creditors. For more information on this aspect, you should consult your legal advisor.

As with any other tax shelter, an investment in an exempt policy should be assessed on its merits. The insurance business is competitive, so you should shop around before making a decision.

Spouse's Canadian dividends

You may elect to include your spouse's taxable Canadian dividends in your income if by so doing you are able to claim or increase your married status tax credit. All of your spouse's dividends must be transferred. You cannot pick and choose to maximize tax savings.

This strategy works because the tax savings that result from increasing your married status tax credit may more than offset the extra tax that you must pay on the dividends, taking into account the reduced tax on dividends as a result of the dividend tax credit described above.

If adding the dividends to your earnings pushes your net income above the threshold at which the Old Age Security clawback (see page 135) begins to take effect, you may be worse off, and should not make the transfer.

Tax Tip

Check to see whether transferring your spouse's Canadian dividends to your tax return will yield significant tax savings. In some cases the saving may amount to several hundred dollars.

Other investment income

Rental properties are a common investment. In some cases, income from an interest in a partnership is reported as investment income.

• Rental income

Net rental income is taxable. To calculate net rental income, current expenses you incur to earn that income are deducted. Most common are interest, heat, electricity, property taxes, water bills, insurance, labour and materials for routine repairs and maintenance, and the cost of advertising for tenants. Condominium management fees are also deductible.

Capital expenditures can be claimed only through the capital cost allowance (CCA) system. Your CCA claim cannot be used to create or increase a loss on the rental property unless the property qualified as a MURB (Multiple Unit Rental Building).

• Partnership income

If you have an interest in a partnership or limited partnership in which you are not actively engaged, you must report your share of net income or loss on Schedule 5 of your tax return. Normally, you receive a tax reporting package from the general partner that sets out the amount. You should attach this information to your tax return.

If you are a limited partner and a portion of a partnership loss is allocated to you, the investment may be a tax shelter subject to the at-risk rules. (See page 110 for more information about at-risk rules and about measures dealing with partnership interests that were introduced in the 1994 federal budget.)

You may deduct partnership losses allocated to you only to the extent of your at-risk amount. This means that you cannot deduct losses that exceed the cost of your interest in the partnership, plus profits (or less losses) and other adjustments.

If you have not received a tax reporting package from the general partner, or are uncomfortable with the calculations required, you should talk to your tax advisor.

Deductible interest expense

In general, interest paid or accrued on funds borrowed to earn investment or business income is deductible for tax purposes.

In this context, investment income includes interest and dividends, as well as other sources of income, such as royalties and "passive" rental income. While investment income in this context does not include capital gains that may be realized on capital property, many investments – such as shares and mutual funds – have the potential of paying dividends or earning income at some future date even if they do not currently. Accordingly, interest expense is generally deductible on funds borrowed to acquire these types of investments.

What happens if you sell the source of your business or property income at a loss? The courts have confirmed that interest ceases to be deductible when the source of income to which the interest related no longer exists or is sold and the borrowed money cannot be traced to a replacement income-producing source.

Fortunately, new rules provide that interest on borrowed money may continue to be deductible even if the source of the income from business or property is no longer held. The new provisions apply when the loss of source of income occurs after 1993.

For example, assume that you borrowed $4,500 in 1992 to acquire shares for your investment portfolio. The shares cost a total of $6,000. The shares decline in value and you sell them for $3,600. You no longer have the shares, but you still owe money to the bank. Under the old rules, the interest on the borrowed funds would no longer be tax-deductible to you.

Under the new rules, and assuming that the shares are sold after 1993, you may be able to continue to deduct all or a portion of your interest expense, depending on what you do with the $3,600 proceeds.

- If you use the $3,600 proceeds to buy another corporation's shares, you will be able to deduct the full amount of your interest on the original borrowing. Here's how it works: since you sold the first shares for 60% of their cost ($6,000–$3,600), $2,700 (60% of your $4,500 original borrowing) is considered to have been used to acquire the new shares. Since you used the proceeds to buy income-producing property, the interest on the $2,700 is tax-deductible. The new rules will deem the balance of the original borrowing, $1,800, to continue to be used to earn income from the first lot of shares. Accordingly, you will be able to continue to deduct interest on the $1,800. The result? You may deduct the full amount of interest on the $4,500 that you borrowed.

- Keep the facts the same as above, but this time you use the $3,600 to pay down your credit card balance. What happens to your interest expense? In the same way as in the scenario above, interest on $1,800 continues to be tax-deductible. Interest on the $2,700, however, is no longer deductible because you used that portion of the borrowed funds for personal reasons and not for an income-producing purpose.

The rules will also apply if you borrowed money for the purpose of earning income from a business and the business ceases after 1993. In this situation, you may continue to deduct all or a portion of the interest on money you borrowed for your business depending on how the business is liquidated.

Tax Tip

If you must borrow, try to borrow for investment or business purposes before you borrow for personal reasons. Conversely, when repaying debt, always repay loans on which interest is non-deductible before you repay those on which the interest is deductible.

Tax Tip

If you are buying Canada Savings Bonds on a payroll savings plan, don't forget to claim a deduction for interest expense. Essentially, you have purchased the bonds at the first of November with borrowed funds and you repay the loan with interest during the year.

Capital gains and losses

Capital gains and losses are realized when you dispose of a property. The word "dispose" is used because you may be subject to special rules that deem you to have disposed of a property under certain circumstances, even if you have not sold the property in the ordinary sense.

A disposition for nil proceeds is deemed to occur when shares have a fair market value of zero, the company is insolvent and has ceased carrying on business, and it is reasonable to expect the corporation to dissolve. No disposition will be deemed to occur if the corporation continues to carry on business within two years of the end of the year.

Property includes real estate, shares in a corporation, an interest in a partnership, depreciable property such as cars or a building, rights or options to purchase or sell property, and even personal property such as antiques, books, or boats.

To the extent that capital gains are not covered by the capital gains exemption (see the next topic) three-quarters of your realized capital gains are subject to tax (two-thirds in 1988 and 1989; one-half prior to 1988). Appendix 3 compares the tax payable on capital gains to that on other forms of income.

Capital losses are multiplied by the same fractions to determine your allowable capital loss. Allowable capital losses realized in the year must first be used to reduce all taxable capital gains realized in the year. Any balance remaining can then be carried back to the three immediately preceding years to reduce taxable capital gains, and any further balance may be carried forward indefinitely and likewise be used to reduce taxable capital gains.

Losses carried back and used to reduce capital gains of prior years may restore a portion of your capital gains exemption previously used.

Realization of significant capital gains may result in liability for alternative minimum tax (AMT). For more details about AMT, see page 177.

Tax Tip

Unused losses that have been carried forward from years before 1985 may be applied at a rate of $2,000 per year to reduce income from any other sources.

Capital gains exemption

The $100,000 lifetime capital gains exemption is finally gone after years of speculation. The 1994 federal budget proposed to eliminate the $100,000 capital gains exemption for gains realized or accrued after February 22, 1994. If you still have capital gains exemption available, however, all may not be lost.

If you realized a capital gain on the sale of property between January 1 and February 21, 1994, you may still shelter the gain with any unused capital gains exemption.

If you sold property for a gain after February 22, 1994, you may make a special election (see below) and shelter a portion of the gain – that which accrued up to February 22, 1994 – with any of the capital gains exemption that is still available to you.

If you owned capital property on February 22, 1994, you may file a special election with your 1994 income tax return. This election will allow you to report a capital gain (even though you did not actually sell your property) and claim the capital gains exemption.

How does it work? When you file the election, you will be treated as having sold your property on February 22, 1994 and having immediately reacquired it. This will allow you to report capital gains that have accrued on the property up to budget day and to claim the exemption on your 1994 income tax return. When the property is sold at a later date, you will add the capital gain that you reported for purposes of the election to the cost of the property. This will reduce any gain in the year of sale and will decrease the tax that you would otherwise have to pay. Any loss will also be based on the elected amount.

For the purposes of the election, you may select the amount that you wish to be the notional proceeds of disposition. The amount that you choose, however, must be greater than the adjusted cost base (ACB) of the property and less than or equal to its fair market value (FMV). Further, the amount must be such that the resulting gain does not exceed the gain that you would otherwise need to recognize to use the capital gains exemption that you have left. For example, if your property has an ACB of $50,000 and a FMV of $200,000 and you have the full $100,000 exemption available to you, you would elect for the deemed proceeds of disposition to be $150,000. This would allow you to shelter the $100,000 capital gain with the $100,000 exemption.

Investors who make an election in respect of depreciable property will not recognize recapture of capital cost allowance (CCA) until the subsequent disposition of the property.

While the $100,000 capital gains exemption in respect of capital gains realized on the disposition of "non-qualifying property" purchased after February 1992 was eliminated, you may still make the election to use your available capital gains exemption in your 1994 return if you own non-qualifying property acquired before that date. Non-qualifying property is generally defined to mean real property that is not used in an active business. Your rental property or your country or vacation home (if they are homes you own in addition to your principal residence) are considered non-qualifying property.

The method of choosing the amount that you will use to make the election on your tax return will be different for non-qualifying property than for other capital property. Because the capital gains exemption in respect of non-qualifying property was eliminated after February 1992, you must use a formula to determine the amount of a gain on the disposition of non-qualifying property that is eligible for the capital gains exemption. Basically, the total gain must be prorated between the periods before March 1992 and after February 1992.

For example, suppose you acquired a non-qualifying property on January 1, 1985 at a cost of $150,000. Assume that the FMV on February 22, 1994 is $400,000 and you have the full capital gains exemption available to you.

At first glance, if would appear logical to elect $250,000 to be the deemed proceeds of disposition, because $250,000 less the ACB of $150,000 produces $100,000 of capital gain, which equals the exemption. Because of the formula, however, only part of the $100,000 gain would be eligible for sheltering with the exemption. In this example, the exemption is $100,000 × 86 months (January 1, 1985 to February 29, 1992) divided by 110 months (total number of months the property was owned up to and including February 1994).

To use the full capital gains exemption, the elected proceeds of disposition should be increased so that elected amount will result in a capital gain that when prorated will equal $100,000. The desired gain is therefore $100,000 × 110/86 = $127,907, and the elected amount should be that amount plus the ACB (i.e., $127,907 + $150,000 = $277,907.)

What happens to the non-eligible portion of the gain? In effect, the $127,907 figure is reduced by a special deduction in respect of the gain, prorated for the period after February, 1992 ($27,907 in this example). The result is a $100,000 capital gain that you report on your tax return, which is added to the ACB of the property. The new ACB of the property would be $250,000 ($150,000 of original ACB plus $100,000 of capital gain). The result is that tax on the non-eligible portion of the gain, (i.e., $27,907) is deferred until you actually dispose of the property. Special rules apply if the property is your principal residence any time after February 22, 1994.

What type of information do you have to compile to make the election? You will need to know the ACB of the property as well as its FMV on February 22, 1994. The ACB of a property usually comprises its original cost (including expenses you paid to buy it such as commissions and legal fees) plus the cost of additions and improvements you made to the property up to February 22, 1994. The FMV of the property is generally the highest dollar value that your property would bring in an open and unrestricted market between a willing buyer and a willing vendor who are acting independently of each other.

Tax Tip

Monitor the capital gains and capital losses that you incur after February 22, 1994. Your ability to claim the capital gains exemption will be eroded if the capital losses that you incur after February 22, 1994 exceed the capital gains that you realize after that date. You may avoid this by delaying the sale of properties with accrued losses until 1995. Or, sell enough properties with accrued gains to offset your capital losses that would otherwise erode your ability to claim the capital gains exemption.

For publicly traded securities, the FMV will ordinarily be the stock-market-quoted value for February 22, 1994. You can find this information from public listings of transactions on recognized stock exchanges, investment publications, or from your broker. The FMV will be more difficult for securities in privately owned businesses. You may have to obtain a valuation from an accountant or a business valuator. As far as real estate is concerned, the FMV can be determined by professional appraisers. You can also get this information yourself from real estate pamphlets, newspapers, and land registry offices. For items such as art, coins, stamps, and jewellery you will probably have to consult with a dealer or an appraiser.

Tax Tip

You should ascertain the FMV of your property as soon as possible. The longer you wait, the more difficult it may be to readily determine its value, particularly for property other than publicly traded securities.

What effect will making the election have on you? Making the election will not increase your taxable income, because reporting the gain will be offset by the capital gains exemption. However, it will increase your net income. This may reduce your child tax benefit, GST credit, guaranteed income supplement, provincial tax credits, and some non-refundable tax credits such as the age amount and medical expenses. Making the election may also subject you to minimum tax, increase some provincial taxes, and require you to repay all or part of any social benefits such as OAS.

Filing the election is optional, so you might want to begin gathering information about the ACB and FMV of your property now and make some preliminary calculations to determine if the election is beneficial to you. You may also want to discuss the ramifications of the election with your professional advisor.

Of course, all of the usual rules regarding the capital gains exemption still apply. You must reduce the exemption that you claim in 1994 by allowable losses for the year and as well as by allowable business investment losses (ABILs), whether realized in Canada or elsewhere. In addition, if you have a cumulative net investment loss (CNIL) balance, it will reduce the amount of the exemption. Corporations and trusts do not qualify, although capital gains flowed to beneficiaries from a trust would be eligible for the exemption. You must be a Canadian resident to claim the exemption. If you were resident in Canada only part of the year, you may still claim the exemption if you were a resident of Canada throughout the immediately preceding year or the following year.

Tax Tip

If you transferred capital property to your spouse and/or children over the last few years in order to use your lifetime capital gains exemption and the property has increased in value, consider whether these family members should make the election to shelter the accrued gains on their 1994 income tax returns. If the election is not made in 1994, the capital gains exemption will be lost to them forever.

The measures proposed in the federal budget do not affect the enhanced capital gains exemption for Qualifying Small Business

Corporation shares and qualified farm property. Gains on a principal residence also remain exempt.

Tax Tip

If you have net capital loss carryovers, or can create a capital loss by selling a particular property, you may be able to shelter the non-exempt portion of a gain realized on the disposition of non-qualifying property.

An additional enhanced $400,000 exemption is available for gains realized on the disposition of shares of a Qualifying Small Business Corporation (QSBC) or on the disposition of a qualified family farm operation.

When the expression "enhanced capital gains exemption" is discussed or referred to in this book, the amount of the exemption will be taken to be $400,000. This assumes that the general lifetime capital gains exemption has already been claimed. For individuals who have not used their $100,000 capital gains exemption in respect of other property, the enhanced exemption will be $500,000.

For the disposition of shares to be eligible for the additional $400,000 exemption, at the time of sale, the company must be a small business corporation (SBC). An SBC is generally defined as a Canadian-controlled private corporation (CCPC) that uses all or substantially all (more than 90%) of the fair market value of its assets in an active business carried on primarily in Canada. Also included are CCPCs whose assets are shares in qualifying SBCs.

Shares of a corporation will not qualify as QSBC shares unless, at the time of sale, all or substantially all of the assets of the corporation are used in active business carried on primarily in Canada by the corporation or a related corporation, and/or shares or debt of "connected" SBCs. Revenue Canada considers this test to be satisfied if at least 90% of the fair market value of the assets fall within this description.

The corporation must also comply with restrictive requirements concerning the nature of its assets throughout the relevant holding period (usually two years prior to the date of sale). More than 50% of the fair market value of the assets must be attributable to assets used in active business carried on by it or a related corporation primarily in Canada and/or shares or debt of connected CCPCs that satisfy certain holding period and asset tests. (See page 73 for the exemption when a business goes public.)

If a disposition is deemed to have occurred as a consequence of a shareholder's death and the corporation fails to meet the "all or substantially all" test immediately before the time of death, the opportunity to use the enhanced $400,000 capital gains exemption that otherwise may have been lost could be protected by a measure that is intended to provide relief in such situations. A share that is deemed to have been disposed of on a shareholder's death may constitute a QSBC share at the time of the disposition if it met the "all or substantially all" test at any time within the 12-month period preceding the disposition.

When a corporation holds a life insurance policy under which a shareholder of that corporation is the life insured, an increase in the value of the policy could cause the corporation to fail the asset tests in the definitions described above. This could result in the enhanced gains exemption not being available on the deemed disposition of the shares on the taxpayer's death. For the purposes of the definitions of a QSBC share and a share of the capital stock of a family farm corporation (see below), a relieving provision deems the fair market value of the policy at any time prior to the shareholder's death to be its cash surrender value.

A farm property qualifying for the enhanced $400,000 exemption may be operated as a corporation or a farm partnership. The property must be actively farmed by the taxpayer or family members immediately before the sale to qualify for the exemption, and all or substantially all the assets of the business must be devoted to farming. To qualify, the property may have to meet holding period requirements similar to those for QSBC shares.

The definition of "share of the capital stock of a family farm corporation" clarifies that the property of a family farm corporation is not required to be used in the course of carrying on the business of farming at the time of the disposition of the share. Provided that the other conditions in the definition have been satisfied, prior use of the property throughout any 24-month period ending before the disposition will suffice. A similar clarification exists for an interest in a family farm partnership.

Tax Tip

Eligible farm property can be transferred to your children at your cost, so there are no immediate adverse tax consequences, unless an AMT liability arises (see page 177). If you are not going to otherwise use your enhanced $400,000 capital gains exemption, consider electing to transfer the property at a higher value and claiming the exemption. This strategy would "step up" your child's cost base for the farm and he or she will be liable for a much smaller capital gain on any eventual sale.

Reserves

If you sell a capital property at a profit and do not receive the full proceeds at the time of sale or before the end of the calendar year, you may be eligible to claim a reserve. The reserve represents the portion of the gain related to the sale proceeds that are not due until after the end of the year. The reserve is available if you secured the unpaid balance of the purchase price by way of a note payable or a mortgage.

The tax on your gain can be postponed for no longer than five years on most types of capital property. (The reserve limit is extended to ten years for qualified farm property or shares in a small business corporation sold to your children, grandchildren, or great grandchildren.) Each year, beginning with the year of sale, you must bring into income the greater of:

- your capital gain times the proportion of the proceeds actually received prior to the end of the year, less the amount previously recognized; and

- one-fifth (or one-tenth, if appropriate) of the capital gain for each year from the year of sale to the current year.

Amounts brought into income each year under the reserve mechanism are treated as capital gains. The amounts to be included in your income are based on the capital gains inclusion rate in effect in the year the reserve is brought into income. A reserve that you bring into income after 1987 and that relates to a disposition after 1984 is eligible for the lifetime capital gains exemption.

If you sold a property before November 13, 1981, and proceeds are still outstanding, the five or ten-year limits on claiming reserves do not apply.

Tax Tip

The 1994 federal budget proposes to eliminate the $100,000 lifetime capital gains exemption for gains realized on dispositions of property after February 22, 1994. If a reserve that is brought into your 1994 income is eligible for the lifetime capital gains exemption, consider claiming less than the maximum reserve for 1994 to fully use your available lifetime capital gains exemption.

Cumulative net investment losses (CNILs)

The CNIL rules were designed to prevent investors from claiming deductions for interest and other investment expenses as well as the capital gains exemption. The elimination of the general lifetime capital gains exemption means that the CNIL will be relevant only in limited circumstances. Net capital gains eligible for the enhanced capital gains exemption on qualifying small business corporation shares or on qualified family farm property, or on capital gains in respect of which an election will be made in your 1994 return, must be reduced by your CNIL. If the capital gains exemption is no longer available to you — because you have exhausted your lifetime exemption or the enhanced exemption or because you did not own property on February 22, 1994 on which you can make the special election — you need not be concerned with the CNIL rules at all.

Tax Tip

Even though the capital gains exemption has effectively been eliminated after February 22, 1994, if you are planning to use the capital gains exemption election in your 1994 return, be careful not to get tripped up by a CNIL balance. Your CNIL will still be calculated to the end of the year. Accordingly, if you (a) have unused capital gains exemption; (b) owned capital property with accrued gains on February 22, 1994 and would otherwise make the election in 1994; but (c) had a CNIL problem at December 31, 1993, you have until the end of 1994 to "cure" your CNIL.

On the other hand, if you believe that you have no CNIL balance and are safe to make the election in respect of gains that accrued to February 22, 1994, be particularly careful that you do not go offside during the rest of the year. If you do, you will lose access to the capital gains exemption forever.

Your CNIL is computed at the end of a year as the amount by which your investment expenses accumulated after 1987 exceed investment income also accumulated after 1987. Investment income includes the following types of income reported on your tax return:

- interest, the taxable amount of dividends, and other income from investments;

- your share of net income from a partnership in which you are not an active member;

- income from property or from the renting or leasing of rental property; and

- 50% of income relating to the recovery of exploration and development expenses.

Investment expenses generally include the following expenses claimed on your tax return:

- interest and carrying charges relating to investments that yield interest, dividends, and rent;

- interest and carrying charges relating to your interest in a partnership in which you are not an active member;

- your share of a loss in a partnership in which you are not an active member;

- 50% of exploration and development expenses claimed; and

- any loss for the year from property or from renting or leasing rental property.

Your interest expense and other eligible investment expenses and losses remain deductible and your access to the enhanced capital gains exemption is merely delayed, not eroded.

For 1992 and subsequent taxation years, your CNIL will be reduced by certain net taxable capital gains in respect of non-qualifying property. This will be achieved by treating the taxable portion of gains on non-qualifying property (i.e., the portion not eligible for the capital gains exemption) as investment income in your CNIL calculation.

Tax Tip

If possible, borrow for business purposes as opposed to investment purposes. The interest expense on funds borrowed to carry on a business or profession does not enter into the calculation of your CNIL account.

Special rules for capital gains and losses

• Identical properties

When you acquire securities that are exactly the same – Class A common shares of ABC Corp. for example – the shares are pooled for purposes of determining your cost when you sell a portion of your holdings.

Assume, for example, that you buy 200 shares today at $5 each (total cost $1,000) and 100 shares next week at $8 each (total cost $800). Your cost per share for tax purposes is $6 (300 shares for a total cost of $1,800). If you then sell 200 shares at $7 each, your capital gain is $200 ($7 minus $6 times 200 shares).

Tax Tip

When determining which of your losers to sell prior to year end, ensure that you have indeed accrued losses on the specific securities and that you will not be tripped up by the identical property rules.

• Pre-1972 capital property

Capital gains were not subject to tax before 1972. If you acquired a property before 1972 and you still own it, the portion of any gain accruing to December 31, 1971 is not subject to tax. To determine the portion of the total post-1971 capital gain, you must know the value of the property on V-Day (Valuation Day, basically December 31, 1971) or you may have to have the property valued as of that date, which could be costly. A published list gives V-Day values for publicly traded securities.

If you own identical properties, some of which were acquired before 1972, on a disposition you will be deemed to have sold the pre-1972 properties before those acquired after 1971. Two separate pools will determine the cost of the properties sold; one comprising the properties acquired before 1972, another for those acquired after 1971.

Tax Tip
Before having a property evaluated for purposes of determining the nontaxable pre-1972 gain, ensure that the cost of the valuation will be more than offset by the expected tax savings.

• Superficial losses
If during the year you realized capital gains that will be taxable, you may be tempted to dispose of some of your losers to offset the gains. In so doing, however, be careful not to run afoul of the superficial loss rules. A superficial loss arises if you repurchase a security identical to the one you disposed of within 30 days before or after the original sale.

A superficial loss will result in the denial of any loss realized on the original sale and the amount of the loss will simply be added to the cost base of the newly acquired identical property. A similar result occurs if your spouse or a corporation that you control purchases the identical security.

• Denial of capital losses
In two specific situations you are not permitted to recognize a loss for tax purposes:

- If you sell capital property to a corporation that is controlled by you or your spouse, the property will be considered to have been transferred to the corporation at your cost, even if you sell the property to the corporation at a loss.

- Losses arising on the sale of capital property to your own or your spouse's RRSP or RRIF will be denied in their entirety. You would be better off selling the property to an arm's length party and making a cash contribution to your RRSP.

• Settlement date

Transactions involving publicly traded securities take place at settlement date: five days after the trading date in the case of Canadian stock exchanges.

Tax Tip

Don't undermine your tax planning strategies by ignoring the settlement date. In 1994, December 21 is probably the last day on which a sale executed through a Canadian stock exchange will be considered a 1994 transaction. Your broker can tell you if foreign exchanges have different settlement dates.

Allowable business investment losses (ABILs)

Losses incurred on the sale of shares or debt in a Small Business Corporation (SBC) are treated differently from ordinary capital losses. An SBC is a Canadian-controlled private corporation (CCPC) that uses all or substantially all of its assets in an active business carried on primarily in Canada, based on a fair market value test. Included are CCPCs whose assets are shares in qualifying SBCs.

An ABIL is calculated in the same manner as an allowable capital loss: three-quarters of the business loss is the ABIL for 1990 and subsequent taxation years.

An ABIL is a reduction in computing net income, unlike an allowable capital loss, which may be used only to reduce taxable capital gains. Any portion of an ABIL not used may be carried back three years and forward seven, the same as normal business losses. After that time, business investment losses become ordinary capital losses.

Bear in mind that:

- Your business investment loss may be reduced by dividends paid after 1971 if you owned the shares before 1972.

- Any ABILs realized will reduce your $400,000 enhanced capital gains exemption. (If you are making the special election in your 1994 return, an ABIL will first reduce or eliminate any general capital gains exemption that you claim.)

Tax Tip

While you should consider delaying the realization of an ABIL until you have exhausted your enhanced capital gains exemption, by delaying the recognition of an ABIL, you may be prepaying tax on other income.

Tax Tip

The allowable portion of losses realized on the disposition of shares or debt in an SBC may qualify as business investment losses and therefore may be offset against income from all sources. Remember, however, that any post-1984 losses reduce your capital gains exemption.

Principal residence

• What is a principal residence?

The home you occupy is your principal residence. It can be a house, condominium, cottage, mobile home, trailer, or even a live-aboard boat – as long as you occupy it for a portion of the year. A principal residence need not be located in Canada.

Included in the definition of principal residence is the land on which it is situated. Only the amount of land necessary to the enjoyment of the home is included in the definition, usually no more than one-half hectare. (A hectare is 10,000 square metres or about one and one-quarter acres.)

Where zoning bylaws required a larger parcel of land to be included with your house at the time of purchase, more than one-half hectare of land may be included in the principal residence definition.

• Capital gain on disposition

Gains on the sale of a principal residence are generally tax-free. The principal residence exemption is available to a family unit (you and your spouse and your unmarried children under the age of 18) on only one home, in any one particular year or part year, for gains arising since the beginning of 1982. (For gains arising after 1972 and before 1982, each individual is entitled to the principal residence exemption for one house.)

• Change in use

If you start to rent out part or all of your principal residence, an election is available to preserve the principal residence status for up to four consecutive years. You must report the rent received, net of out-of-pocket expenses, as income. If you claim capital cost allowance (depreciation) on the home while it is being rented, Revenue Canada will consider that you have rescinded the election and deem a disposition to have occurred.

In addition, to claim the principal residence designation, you must continue to be a Canadian resident for the period during which you do not occupy the home.

Foreign residences

Any home that you normally occupy, even on a seasonal basis for only part of the year, may qualify as your principal residence – and this includes a home in another country. You must be a Canadian resident in the years in which you designate your foreign home as your principal residence.

Even though the gain under Canadian rules is tax-free, you may incur a foreign tax liability when you sell your foreign home.

Tax Tip

If you estimate that the foreign tax liability will be significant and that you will be entitled to foreign tax credits on your Canadian tax return for foreign taxes paid, you may be better off not claiming the principal residence exemption. Professional advice is essential in this situation.

• Farm property

A farm house is eligible for the principal residence exemption. When you sell the farm, you may prorate the proceeds between the farming property and your principal residence, including no more than one-half hectare of land as part of your principal residence. Alternatively, you may elect to reduce the full amount of the gain on disposition by $1,000 plus another $1,000 for each year of ownership after 1971.

Tax shelters

Tax shelters are investments or business opportunities that offer various types of income tax savings in addition to the potential economic benefits of a successful investment. In most cases, initial tax savings will be offset by long-term realization of income, if the investment is successful. If the investment does not succeed, the initial tax savings may compensate for part of the economic loss.

The federal government applies specific provisions to restrict or eliminate the benefits of tax-shelter investments, including at-risk rules for limited partnerships, reporting requirements for tax shelter promoters, and capital cost allowance (CCA) restrictions. Other measures may reduce or limit the tax value of tax shelters for some

110   investors. For example, the alternative minimum tax (AMT) limits the benefit of "tax preferences", and cumulative net investment loss (CNIL) rules reduce the amount of the capital gains exemption that may be claimed in a particular year.

Every promoter of a tax shelter is required to obtain an identification number from Revenue Canada. Prior to investing in a new tax shelter, you should confirm that an identification number has been obtained in order to preserve your right to the deductions available to reduce your taxes.

Tax Tip

Evaluate the investment potential of a tax shelter in the same way as any other investment. It does not make any economic sense to invest in a shelter if there is little chance of either earning income on your investment or recovering the amount you have at risk, i.e., the amount you invested net of the tax benefits.

Limited partnerships – at-risk rules

Special rules define and limit the extent to which limited partners can use partnership losses and investment tax credits to shelter other income. Losses of a partnership allocated to a limited partner are deductible only to the extent of the partner's at-risk amount at the end of a particular year. A limited partner's at-risk amount at any time is essentially the cost of his or her partnership interest, plus profits or minus drawings and losses, and other adjustments.

The 1994 federal budget proposed changes that extend the partnership at-risk rules.

The adjusted cost base (ACB) of property that you own reflects your cost of the property and is taken into account in computing a capital gain or loss when you sell the property. In certain circumstances, the ACB of your property may become negative, in which case you would be treated as having realized a capital gain. This rule, however, generally does not apply if the property is a partnership interest. The exception to the rule recognizes that a partner's negative ACB may result from legitimate, and possibly temporary, circumstances, for example, when losses of the partnership are allocated to a partner for tax purposes.

Some tax shelters have been structured to use the exception to the negative ACB rules. To ensure that the at-risk rules cannot be circumvented, the budget proposes that limited partners and certain other passive partners be required to report as a capital gain any negative ACB in their partnership interest at the end of a fiscal period of the partnership.

Although the new rules will apply to fiscal periods of partnerships ending after February 22, 1994, transitional rules will defer the application of the new rules to the fifth fiscal period of the partnership ending after 1994 in the case of film partnerships satisfying certain criteria.

Real estate

Investment in real estate as a tax shelter is not as attractive as it was in the past, because rental losses on real estate cannot be created or increased by claiming capital cost allowance (CCA). In addition, most costs related to the construction period of a project, particularly property taxes and interest expense, must be added to the cost of the land or building and therefore become deductible as depreciation over time, at best, rather than in the first year or two of the investment. Certain soft costs, however, such as rental commissions, guarantees, and landscaping may be deductible in the early years of a project.

Canadian films

Capital cost allowance (CCA) in respect of investments in certified films is limited to a rate of 30% on a declining-balance basis. The rule that normally limits CCA to half the amount that you could otherwise claim in the year of acquisition does not apply. Additional CCA may be claimed up to the lesser of the undepreciated capital cost of certified film productions and the income (net of expenses and the basic 30% CCA) from all certified productions in the year.

The 1994 federal budget proposed some changes to the capital cost allowance rules for films and video tapes.

Some film limited partnerships have raised debt that is convertible into interests in the partnership. After the tax benefits and cash distributions have been allocated to the original limited partners, the lender converts its loan into a partnership interest. In effect, proceeds from the convertible loans are used to acquire films or video tapes at a capital cost that is in excess of the amount that would otherwise be allocated to the limited partners if the lender were considered to be a partner from the time the loan was made.

The budget proposal will reduce the capital cost of a film or video tape by the amount of any loan that is convertible into an interest in the film or a partnership that holds the film or video tape until the convertible loan is exchanged for a partnership interest or is repaid.

Transitional rules will defer the application of the new provisions if certain prospectus-like documents were filed before February 22, 1994 (including offering memoranda distributed but not filed before that date) if the funds are raised before 1995 and expended pursuant to the terms of the documents before 1995 (before March 1995 in the case of certified Canadian productions). Transitional relief is also provided to defer the application of the new rules when the principal photography of certain film productions is completed before 1995 (before March 1995 in the case of certified Canadian productions).

Farming

The attractiveness of a farm shelter from a tax point of view lies primarily in the potential for claiming losses against other sources of income. The key to a farm shelter is the business aspect: to deduct any loss at all, you must have a reasonable expectation of earning a profit from the farming operation. If farming is not at the centre of your livelihood, you may be restricted to $8,750 of losses in a year.

Qualified farm property may be eligible for the enhanced $400,000 capital gains exemption.

Provincial tax shelters

A number of provinces encourage investment in specified areas or industries through various incentive initiatives. Stock savings plans provide tax deductions or credits and venture capital programs are intended to foster investment in small to medium-sized corporations.

Income splitting

Income splitting is having income that normally would be taxed in the hands of the highest income family member taxed at lower rates in the hands of another family member. Tax may even be eliminated if the family member has very little or no income. If you earn income that is taxed at a top marginal rate of say 48% and can arrange to have your spouse earn some of the income so that it is taxed at say 28%, your family will save $20 for every $100 of income earned. Not surprisingly, rules have been established to limit the circumstances in which these transfers may be effective.

Attribution rules

A variety of rules discourage income splitting. Essentially, if you transfer or loan assets to your spouse or a child under 18 years of age, in virtually any manner, the investment income (including interest, dividends, rental income, etc.) will be taxed in your hands, rather than in the hands of your spouse or child. As well, capital gains or losses realized by your spouse on the sale of transferred property will be attributed to you. Attribution of capital gains does not apply on assets transferred to children under 18 years old.

Attribution continues to apply when assets are substituted for the original assets transferred. However, income earned on reinvested income is not attributed to the transferor (see Income on income, page 116).

While attribution of income ordinarily ceases when a child turns 18, income earned on an investment made by a child age 18 or over (or any other non-arm's length person) using borrowed funds is subject to the attribution rules if one of the main reasons for the loan is to reduce or avoid tax by having the investment income taxed in the child's hands.

The attribution rules may apply not only to loans, but to all situations in which an individual becomes indebted to another non-arm's-length individual. Accordingly, the attribution rules will apply when, for example, the unpaid balance of a purchase price is satisfied by a non-interest-bearing note and one of the main reasons for incurring the indebtedness was to avoid tax by having income included in the hands of the debtor.

In spite of the attribution rules, a number of ways to split income among family members still work. For example, business income is not attributed, neither is income that results if a loan is made at commercial interest rates and the interest is actually paid within 30 days of year end. Similarly, sales to a spouse at fair market value are not subject to the rules if you receive adequate consideration in return. Since transfers of property between spouses are generally considered to be made at the adjusted cost base of the property, if you want to use this strategy, you must elect on your tax return that the transfer take place at fair market value rather than at the adjusted cost base. And a contribution to a spousal RRSP is still one of the best income-splitting techniques.

If you are in a higher marginal tax bracket than your spouse, you might consider paying off any balances on your spouse's credit cards. The attribution rules will not apply as long as the credit card debt was not used to acquire income-producing property.

Gifts

If your income is taxed at a higher marginal tax rate than your spouse's, the family will benefit if your spouse earns investment income and you pay family expenses such as credit card balances. Although these payments could be considered gifts to your spouse, no attribution would apply, since the funds are used to pay ordinary costs of running a family and not to generate investment income.

Tax Tip
Investment income may be shifted to a child 18 or over by an outright sale or gift of the income-producing property.

Tax Tip
Since capital gains on property transferred to children under 18 years of age are not attributed, consider buying capital property with a low yield but high capital gains potential in the names of your children. The income will be attributed to you, but any future capital gains will be taxed in the children's hands, presumably at lower tax rates.

116 | Income on income

Income earned on property that you transfer to your spouse or a child under 18 is generally subject to the income attribution rules and is included in your income for tax purposes. If, however, he or she reinvests the income, income earned on the reinvested income (e.g., interest on interest) is not attributed to you.

Common-law spouse

Two individuals of opposite sex are considered to be spouses of each other when they are cohabiting in a conjugal relationship and they either:

• have so cohabited throughout the preceding 12 months; or

• are the parents of the same child.

Common-law couples are eligible for the married tax credit and may make contributions to spousal RRSPs. Common-law couples are subject to the attribution rules and many other provisions that apply to married couples, including rules that deny losses on the disposition of property to a spouse. Common-law spouses must combine their incomes for the purposes of determining the GST tax credit and the monthly payments under the Child Tax Benefit system (see page 180). The deductibility of child care expenses may be adversely affected. A common-law couple is subject to the same rules that limit a married couple or a family unit to one principal residence.

How does the government monitor common-law couples who choose not to live by the new rules? When does a common-law relationship begin and end? While marriage, divorce, and separation are legally defined by registration, divorce decrees, separation agreements, etc., whether two people are in a common-law relationship is often unclear. They may even disagree between themselves.

Common-law couples must be careful that they do not fail to anticipate the substantial income tax consequences that may arise as a result of the conduct of their private lives. For example, a legally married individual who leaves his or her spouse, begins living with another person and has a child with that person, may not only have two spouses, but may also inherit an unusually large group of related persons.

Investment holding companies

The tax system contains special rules that are meant to eliminate some of the biases between income earned by an individual and income earned by a corporation. Some of these are designed to ensure that the after-tax return on income realized through a corporation, and subsequently distributed to the shareholder, is roughly the same as if the shareholder had received the income from the investments directly. The system is imperfect, because surtaxes are imposed on individuals in certain provinces and provincial income tax rates vary. In any case, earning interest, dividends, and capital gains in a corporation is usually advantageous as long as the income is retained in the corporation and the second incidence of tax on distribution is postponed.

There is a small tax cost when the corporate tax, net of partial refunds, is added to the additional tax payable by an individual on receipt of dividends from his or her holding company. Accordingly, based solely on taxation, you would invest directly if you want the income in your own hands immediately, and through a holding company if you can forego the cash income for a while.

Another significant factor is that the enhanced capital gains exemption is available only to individuals. Capital property eligible for the enhanced capital gains exemption that might appreciate in the future should be held personally, at least to a level sufficient to use the full exemption. To take advantage of the enhanced capital gains exemption, you might sell for fair market value assets that you hold personally and that have appreciated in value to your holding company. This tactic offers two main benefits: you could realize a capital gain that would be sheltered by the enhanced capital gains exemption and give the corporation an increased cost base; and the company would hold an asset that may earn income at a lower tax cost.

On the other hand, the tax benefits of using a holding company may not be great, and associated costs may suggest that you wind up your company. Liquidating your holding company may mean that you can use the enhanced capital gains exemption in the future. However, costs are associated with a liquidation, such as taxes on accrued gains and the distributed dividend, as well as legal and accounting fees. Also, maintaining the corporate structure may provide benefits such as opportunities for income splitting and estate planning.

Whether an individual would benefit from using a holding company will depend on the particular circumstances. You should seek professional advice if you are contemplating either establishing or dismantling an investment holding company.

Tax Tip

You can use an investment holding company as a discretionary source of dividend income to reduce the balance in your cumulative net investment loss (CNIL) account if and when necessary.

International investors

Canadians investing outside Canada

Canadian residents are taxed on their worldwide incomes. Accordingly, income you earn on investments made in foreign jurisdictions is subject to tax in Canada and must be reported on your income tax return. Whether the funds are deposited into your Canadian bank account or into a bank account in a foreign country is irrelevant.

Generally, you may use the average exchange rate for the year to convert to Canadian dollars both the amount of income to be reported on your tax return and the amount of foreign tax withheld. However, you may use the actual rates at the time the income was received if that is more beneficial. Tax may be withheld in the foreign country from funds remitted to you. You must include the gross amount of earnings, i.e., the amount you received plus the withholding tax. The 25% dividend gross-up rule does not apply, nor is a dividend tax credit available in respect of non-Canadian dividends.

Any foreign tax withheld (up to 15% of the gross foreign investment income) should be used in the foreign tax credit calculation to determine the amount of foreign tax that may be deducted from your Canadian tax liability. Foreign tax withheld in excess of 15% may be deducted in arriving at net income for tax purposes.

Foreign source investment income is subject to the same reporting requirements as Canadian investment income, i.e., interest income accrued but not received must be included in income on an annual basis for investments acquired after 1989 (at least every three years for pre-1990 investments).

Tax Tip

A foreign tax credit may be claimed only when amounts are actually paid and foreign taxes withheld. Consequently, no foreign tax credits may be claimed in respect of investment income accrued but not received. Consider filing a waiver with Revenue Canada to keep "open" years in which unpaid interest is reported. This should ensure that the related foreign tax credit will be allowed when amounts are actually received. Be careful to limit the waiver, which is filed on Form T2029, to the accrued investment income reported.

🌏 Non-resident investors in Canada

If you are a non-resident of Canada receiving income from Canadian sources, you may be subject to federal tax in Canada.

If you receive passive investment income such as interest, dividends, royalties, rents, and pensions, you are not ordinarily required to file a Canadian income tax return. Instead, the Canadian payor of these types of income is required to pay tax on your behalf by withholding and remitting the appropriate amount of tax at source. The general rate of withholding tax on payments to non-residents is 25%, but the rate may be reduced to between zero and 20%, depending on the type of income and whether a bilateral tax treaty is in force between Canada and the country in which you reside.

If you are a non-resident of Canada and you received certain types of income (for example, alimony payments, pension or super-annuation benefits, retiring allowances, RRSP, or RRIF payments) that are otherwise subject to the withholding of tax at source, you may elect to file a Canadian income tax return if the tax reported would be less than the amount withheld. If you do, the election must be made within six months of the end of the calendar year, and you must report all income from Canadian sources. You may generally claim deductions that relate to income reported on the return. In addition, you may be able to claim personal tax credits (see below). Any Canadian tax that has been withheld from income reported on this elective return will be refunded to you if your return shows an overpayment of tax.

Personal tax credits are generally available to an electing non-resident only if more than half of the individual's income is taxable income earned in Canada. In addition, the amount of credits that may be claimed is limited. If you receive rental income from Canada, withholding tax is imposed on the gross amount of rent. You may, however, elect to file a Canadian income tax return and report the rental income and claim related expenses (including capital cost allowance). Again, you would make this election if it reduced your tax liability. You may not claim any other deductions or personal tax credits (i.e., the only income and expenses reported on this type of return must be related to the rental property). However, there is a catch: you will have to file a return for the year in which you dispose of the property and pay tax on any recaptured depreciation or taxable capital gains.

A non-resident of Canada is also subject to Canadian tax on dispositions of taxable Canadian property. Taxable Canadian property includes, among other things, real property (land and buildings, for example), capital property used in carrying on business in Canada, shares of a private corporation that is resident or deemed to be resident in Canada, and shares of a public corporation if at any time during the five years immediately preceding the disposition the non-resident and persons with whom he or she did not deal at arm's length owned 25% or more of the issued shares of any class of its capital stock.

A non-resident will use the same rules to determine taxable capital gains and allowable capital losses as a Canadian resident. Although non-residents are not generally subject to provincial income tax, a federal surtax applies to income earned outside a province. The rate is 52% of basic federal tax.

Tax Tip

If you are a non-resident considering investing in Canada, depending on the type of investment and the magnitude of funds to be invested, you may benefit from holding your investment through a corporation, rather than directly. You should discuss your plans with your professional advisor.

Tax Tip

If you are a non-resident and plan to become a resident of Canada, consider seeking professional advice regarding opportunities to minimize or defer tax as well as potential liabilities to avoid in the course of relocation.

122   ## ⚜ Québec

If you are an investor resident in Québec, the comments above apply for Québec tax purposes, except for the following:

Investment income

You may claim a Québec dividend tax credit of 11.08% of the actual amount of dividends (equivalent to 8.87% of the grossed–up amount) in the calculation of your Québec taxes.

Capital gains or losses

Unused losses that have been carried forward from years before 1985 may be applied at a rate of $1,000 per year to reduce income from any other source.

Cumulative net investment losses (CNILs)

To encourage Québec investments, Québec excludes from the calculation of CNIL deductions for:

- the Québec stock savings plan (QSSP);

- the Cooperative investment plan (CIP);

- Québec business investment companies (QBIC);

- R&D venture capital corporations;

- exploration expenses incurred in Québec; and

- the additional deduction for Québec exploration.

If the foreign tax credit that may be claimed in calculating your federal tax liability is limited, the balance could be claimed in the calculation of your Québec income taxes. Foreign tax withheld in excess of 15% may be deducted in arriving at net income for tax purposes. Note that for Québec purposes, the strategy of filing a waiver to keep open years in which unpaid interest is reported (see Tax Tip regarding foreign tax credits on page 109) may not be possible. It is Revenue Québec's position that waivers to keep years "open" can only be initiated by the Minister of Revenue of Québec.

Non-resident investors in Canada

Special elections allowed under federal tax legislation dealing with:

- certain types of income (for example, alimony payments, pension or superannuation benefits, retiring allowances, RRSP, or RRIF payments); or

- rental income received by a non-resident of Canada,

have no application for Québec tax purposes since no Québec tax is withheld at source.

For Québec tax purposes, any individual who has not resided in Canada at any time during the year but who has:

- been employed in Québec;

- conducted a business in Québec; or

- disposed of a taxable Québec property during the year,

will generally be subject to Québec tax. In such a case, the federal surtax of 52% of basic federal tax that normally applies to income earned outside a province is not applicable.

Québec tax shelters

Québec encourages investment in specified areas or industries through various incentive initiatives. Stock savings plans provide tax deductions and venture capital programs are intended to foster investment in small to medium-sized corporations.

The following are considered to be "Québec tax shelters":

- the Québec stock savings plan (QSSP);

- the Cooperative investment plan (CIP);

- Québec business investment companies (QBIC);

- R&D venture capital corporations; and

- exploration expenses incurred in Québec.

• Québec stock savings plan (QSSP)

A taxpayer who:

- is resident in Québec on the last day of a taxation year; and

- has acquired qualifying shares,

may deduct a portion of the cost of the shares in computing taxable income. The 1994 Québec budget introduced an amendment to the QSSP rules specifying that the last day of the contemplated taxation year is December 31, and not any other taxation year end presumed under special provisions of tax legislation, particularly when a tax payer ceases to reside in Canada. This change applies as of the 1994 taxation year.

Qualifying shares must be purchased no later than December 31. The deductible portion of the cost of qualifying shares is known as the "adjusted cost" and does not include brokerage, safekeeping, or loan fees related to the shares. The adjusted cost of shares corresponds to a deduction varying between 50% and 100% of the actual cost of the shares, depending on the type of corporation, type of shares, and type of investor.

An additional deduction of 50% or 100% is available for QSSP Film shares and QSSP R&D shares (corporations that agree to transfer the value of some tax credits to their shareholders), but the total deductions granted for QSSP shares can never exceed 200%.

The deduction that may be claimed each year with respect to QSSP shares is limited to 10% of "total income". In this context "total income" means net income minus the capital gains deduction claimed in the year.

• Cooperative investment plan (CIP)

Rules for the deduction for shares of a cooperative investment plan (CIP) are similar to those for shares in a QSSP. Employees of a cooperative who purchase shares in their cooperative under a CIP may benefit from a 100% deduction. An additional deduction of 25% is available for investments made after May 2, 1991 under specific programs. Also, an additional 25% will be given for special qualified plans in place after May 16, 1989, raising the deduction levels to 125% or 150%.

Amendments proposed in the 1993 Québec budget will be made so that eligible CIP investors also include individuals employed by a partnership in which an eligible cooperative that issues securities eligible for a CIP holds an interest at the time of issue, if the cooperative's share in the revenues or losses of the partnership exceeds 50%.

• Québec business investment companies (QBICs)

Québec business investment companies (QBICs) are special financing vehicles whose activities consist of investing in small and medium-sized private corporations. A QBIC must be registered as such with the Société de développement industriel du Québec (SDI).

A taxpayer who purchases ordinary shares with full voting rights in a QBIC is entitled to a deduction equal to the lesser of:

- 30% of total income; and

- 125% of the amount invested.

The deduction can reach 150% when a QBIC makes an investment in a designated region. Also, if you are an eligible employee of the corporation in which the investment is made, the deduction will be raised to 150% or 175%, depending on whether or not the investment is made in a designated region.

Higher deductions are available when a QBIC invests in R&D projects or finances Québec films or television productions, but the total deductions granted for QBIC shares can never exceed 200%.

Any amount not claimed in the year may be carried forward to the five subsequent taxation years.

• R&D venture capital corporations

A basic deduction of 100% of the cost of the share will be granted to shareholders of an R&D venture capital corporation when the scientific research and experimental development expenditure is made by or on behalf of the eligible corporation. The basic deduction is limited to 30% of total income.

In addition, a further deduction will be granted to shareholders of the R&D venture capital corporation when the eligible corporation has foregone its Québec tax credits, according to the principle underlying the rules that currently apply for R&D/QSSP vehicles. The additional deduction will be at a rate of 50% or 100%. The higher rate applies if the corporation is entitled to a 50% deduction in respect of wages. Any unused deduction may be carried forward into the five subsequent taxation years.

• Exploration expenses incurred in Québec

To maintain and enhance tax incentives of strategic importance to Québec's economy, the Québec government permits a 25% deduction (reduced from 33⅓% for investments registered before May 15, 1992) with respect to certain exploration expenses incurred in

Québec (in addition to the 100% regular deduction). An additional deduction of 50% (increased from 33⅓% for investments registered before May 15, 1992) can be obtained for mining surface exploration expenses.

• New scientific research and experimental development measures
Scientific research and experimental development will no longer give rise to an additional deduction for the purposes of the QSSP, QBICs, and R&D venture capital corporations. This measure is effective April 23, 1993.

Retired Persons

Retired Persons

Retirement is no longer simple to define. Even if you are actively working and earning income, you should read this chapter if you (or your spouse) receive any pension or similar income, or are 64 years old or older. If you are a director of a corporation and are earning directors' fees, those fees are considered to be employment income and must be included on your tax return. Accordingly, you should glance through the chapter dealing with employees to see if anything pertains to you. For example, if you or your spouse are less than 71 years of age, directors' fees are considered to be earned income for the purposes of determining how much you can contribute to your or a spousal RRSP. Refer to page 198 as well for a discussion concerning directors' liability.

Pension income

You must include in income for tax purposes all of the following payments received during the year:

- benefits from your registered retirement savings plans (RRSPs), whether in the form of periodic payments or a lump sum payment;

- amounts received under your registered retirement income funds (RRIFs);

- income from an annuity;

- superannuation or pension benefits;

- Old Age Security (OAS) benefits;

- Canada Pension Plan (CPP) or Québec Pension Plan (QPP) benefits;

- benefits from a deferred profit sharing plan (DPSP);

- foreign pensions;

- retiring allowances; and

- death benefits.

You may transfer a retiring allowance tax-free to your RRSP, but the amount transferred is restricted to $2,000 per year of service plus $1,500 for each year of service before 1989 for which you were not a member of an RPP or a DPSP.

A death benefit is generally an amount paid to a spouse or other beneficiary in recognition of the deceased's employment service. If you received a death benefit, you must include the amount received in your income. If the deceased person was your spouse, $10,000 of death benefits are exempt from tax. If you received part of the death benefit in one year and the balance in the next, you may still deduct only $10,000 in total.

You may make tax-free transfers of lump sum amounts from an RPP or DPSP to your RRSP (provided the amounts are transferred directly). However, periodic retirement or pension payments cannot be transferred to an RRSP tax-free.

You may also contribute a lump sum amount received from a U.S. Individual Retirement Account (IRA) to your own RRSP or RPP.

Registered retirement savings plans (RRSPs)

You must arrange to receive a retirement income stream from the funds accumulated in your RRSP by the end of the year in which you turn 71. If you do not, your RRSP will be deregistered in the following year and the entire amount will be included in income and taxed at your normal tax rates.

By converting your RRSP into a program that provides you with retirement income, the tax shelter benefits of an RRSP are partially retained. Only the amount you actually receive each year is included in your income. Generally, you have two options.

- You can arrange to receive a life or a fixed-term annuity. The fixed-term annuity extends to age 90 and may be based on your age or your spouse's age if he or she is younger than you. Various issuers may offer different features and prices, so allow yourself some time in your 70th year for shopping around, when the time comes to convert to an annuity.

Both types of annuities may be indexed in a variety of ways so that payments increase each year. Life annuities may be guaranteed for specific periods. Joint annuities based on the lives of both you and your spouse may be arranged. You can also purchase an annuity that may be commuted at your option.

- You can choose to establish a registered retirement income fund (RRIF) with the funds accumulated in your RRSP (see below).

Registered retirement income funds (RRIFs)

An RRIF is a vehicle designed to allow for the tax-free accumulation of earnings in much the same way your RRSP does. Instead of contributing funds to an RRIF, however, the RRIF makes payments to you. Here's how it works.

Transfers from an RPP as well as an RRSP may be made to an RRIF of which you are the annuitant. Transfers from an RPP to an RRIF of which your spouse is the annuitant will also qualify if your spouse became the annuitant as a result of marriage breakdown or your death.

You may have more than one RRIF and you may transfer funds from an RPP or RRSP to your RRIF plans at any time. Since your RRSP must mature (i.e., must be converted to some type of retirement income stream) by the end of the year in which you turn age 71, that is technically the latest time that you can transfer funds from your RRSP to an RRIF. You may also contribute a refund of premiums from a deceased spouse's RRSP to an RRIF tax free.

The RRIF rules allow payments to continue until the death of the annuitant or his or her spouse. While a specific minimum amount must be paid to you each year, (and taxed in your hands, of course), you may withdraw as much as you want at any time. For example, if

you set up an RRIF in the year in which you become 71, you would **133**
have to receive payments equal to at least 7.38% of the value in the
first year. In the second year you would take 7.48% of the value,
and so on.

The minimum percentages that must be withdrawn increase each
year until the annuitant (or his or her spouse) reaches the age of 94.
For years following, the minimum payment is 20% of the value of
the fund at the beginning of each year.

The rules apply to all RRIFs to which funds are transferred after
the end of 1992. For most RRIFs that were purchased before the end
of 1992 ("qualifying RRIFs"), lower minimum payment percentages
apply for ages up to 77. The new minimum payment percentages
(which are lower than those that applied under the old rules) apply
to all RIFFs for ages above 77, regardless of the date of purchase.

RRIFs may also be established before age 71. In that case, the
minimum withdrawal amount will continue to be based on your
current age to age 90.

Of course, the payments you receive are taxable in your hands.
You may have a self-directed RRIF, a mutual fund RRIF, or an
RRIF that guarantees to pay a specific interest rate over the life of
the plan.

Tax Tip

If you have an RRIF from which you receive minimum annual payments based on your age, and you have a spouse who is
younger, consider setting up a new RRIF. Minimum payments
from the new RRIF can then be based on your spouse's age.
The payments will be smaller but will stretch out over more
years. (You may not alter the terms of your current RRIF to
accommodate the smaller payments.) The minimum payments
are just that; you can choose to take out more.

Tax Tip

If you are receiving OAS benefits, withdrawals from your RRSP or payments from an RRIF may subject you to the OAS clawback (see pages 135 and 178).

Pension income credit

The pension income tax credit is 17% of pension income or qualified pension income, depending on your age. The federal credit is limited to $170, which translates into $1,000 of pension income. If you are age 65 or over, pension income includes periodic payments from pension plans (including foreign funds or plans), annuities, profit sharing plans, RRSPs, and RRIFs.

If you are under age 65, you may be eligible for the pension income credit if you receive qualified pension income. Qualified pension income includes life annuity payments from a superannuation or pension plan and certain amounts received as a consequence of the death of your spouse (including a common-law spouse): payments from an RRSP, RRIF or DPSP. Lump sum payments do not qualify in any event, nor do CPP or OAS benefits.

The pension income tax credit is transferable to your spouse if you are unable to use all or a portion of it.

Age credit

You are entitled to claim an age credit if you are age 65 or over. The federal age credit is $592 in 1994, which is 17% of the "age amount" of $3,482.

The federal budget proposes that the age credit be subject to an income test. The age amount will be reduced by 7.5% of your net income exceeding $25,921 in 1994 and by 15% in subsequent years. The reduction is to be phased in over two years. In 1994 the reduction stops when the age amount (and hence the credit) is cut in half. After that, the reduction continues until the age amount and the credit disappear. Accordingly, if your income is over $49,134, you will lose one half of the age credit in 1994 and will not be able to claim the age credit at all in 1995 and subsequent taxation years.

The age amount will not be reduced if the credit is transferred from your spouse.

Old Age Security [OAS] clawback

All taxpayers with net income above $53,215 in 1994 must repay all or a portion of Old Age Security benefits received during the year. The repayment is accomplished by means of a special tax calculated as the lesser of OAS benefits received during the year and 15% of your net income (before deducting the clawback) in excess of $53,215.

The OAS clawback rules have three facets:

- you must include the full amount of OAS benefits received in the year in calculating your income for tax purposes;

- the special tax described above is deductible in arriving at your net income; and

- the special tax is added to your federal and provincial tax payable.

The $53,215 threshold is indexed in the same way as personal tax credits and tax brackets.

Tax Tip

If you are just over the $53,215 threshold and your spouse's net income is below it, consider splitting your CPP benefits if that will bring your net income below $53,215.

Tax Tip

If you are considering making the election to include all of your spouse's taxable Canadian dividends in your income (see page 87), ensure that in so doing you are not subjecting yourself to the OAS clawback.

Foreign pensions

A foreign pension, including a pension from a U.S. Individual Retirement Account (IRA), must be included in your income and is therefore subject to tax in the same way as a Canadian pension.

Canada has social security agreements with a number of countries. These agreements coordinate benefits from each country and are intended to ensure that an individual is not subject to social security taxes of two countries. If you receive a pension from a country with which Canada has entered into a social security agreement, the taxation of your pension benefits may be affected, and you should either seek professional advice or contact your local Health and Welfare Canada office for further information.

If you receive retirement or survivor's benefits under the U.S. Social Security Act, only one-half of the amount need be included in your income. The first $1,000 that is included in your income is also eligible for the pension income credit (see page 134). Moreover, if you are a Canadian resident receiving U.S. social security benefits and are not a U.S. citizen, the benefits are not subject to U.S. tax. (This exemption does not apply to a U.S. citizen who is a resident of Canada.)

Special expenses

Retirement does not trigger any unusual tax treatment of expenses that some retired people may face. However, the credit for medical expenses may apply more broadly than many people realize. In addition to payments to medical practitioners, payments for prescription drugs and various medical aids, the costs of one full-time attendant at home, full-time care in a nursing home, travelling expenses to obtain medical treatment in your area, and home renovation costs to enable you to get around at home may be deductible.

Québec

If you are a retired person resident in Québec, you should be aware that Québec has fully harmonized its legislation with the federal pension reform. In addition, Québec has entered into social security agreements with a number of countries.

Health services fund contribution

For more information about this new contribution, please refer to page 53.

Separated or Divorced Persons

Separated or Divorced Persons

People who are separated or divorced face a special set of tax issues. Those who anticipate separation or divorce must deal with issues that will have tax consequences for many years. These involve the possible distribution of property to satisfy family law requirements, as well as alimony and maintenance payments, income attribution rules, personal tax credits, retirement savings arrangements, and the family's principal residence.

This chapter deals first with issues regarding past marriage breakdowns, and then with issues that are important at the time of marriage breakdown.

For income tax purposes, the definition of "spouse" has been extended to include a common-law spouse. Two persons of the opposite sex will be considered to be spouses of each other if they are cohabiting in a conjugal relationship and either: (a) have so cohabited throughout the preceding 12 months; or (b) are the parents of the same child. The rules extend to common-law couples the application of a broad range of provisions in the *Income Tax Act* that govern the fiscal relations between spouses.

The rule means that common-law spouses are entitled to the married status tax credit and are permitted to contribute to spousal RRSPs. It also means that the attribution rules apply, and that common-law spouses must combine their incomes for purposes of the GST credit and the Child Tax Benefit.

The ramifications of the definition may not be entirely clear for some time. The provisions contain terminology that may give rise to some contentious issues. Accordingly, the fact-gathering process for planning may be far more complex and possibly more delicate. Further, there may be some unintended or unpredictable consequences, since the term "spouse" is used in numerous places in the *Income Tax Act*.

For simplicity, in this chapter "spouse" includes a former spouse.

In the past few years, the tax rules regarding alimony and maintenance payments have been redefined, largely as a result of court cases. The spouse making payments and the spouse receiving payments are both affected. Changes in the family law of several provinces have also contributed to the complexities involved in the division of assets on marriage breakdown.

Tax Tip

Counsel provided by a professional tax advisor may be as important on the breakdown of a marriage as legal advice from a divorce lawyer. The repercussions of failing to consider tax issues involved in a divorce or separation agreement can be very costly.

After marriage breakdown

Alimony and maintenance

Alimony or maintenance payments you make to your spouse are deductible for tax purposes if they meet certain criteria. Conversely, if your spouse can deduct payments to you, you must include them in your income. In general, the reverse is also true: if your spouse cannot deduct the payment, you need not include it in your income.

To be deductible, payments must:

- be periodic (lump sum payments do not qualify, even if made by instalment);

- be for the maintenance of the spouse and/or children; and

- generally be made pursuant to a decree, court order, or judgement, or pursuant to a written agreement.

In addition, the spouses must be living apart at the time payment is made and throughout the remainder of the year.

The recipient must have complete discretion over how the payments are to be used, except in the case of third-party payments (e.g., mortgage payments made directly to a bank) and payments singled out in the divorce or separation agreement to be devoted to a particular use. Generally, the amount of the payment must be specified, although indexed payments may qualify for a deduction as may certain third-party payments of no specific amount. Indexed payments will qualify only if the formula for adjustment is an acceptable one (for example, payments adjusted in accordance with changes in the Consumer Price Index).

Periodic payments made before the date of a court order or written agreement are generally deductible to the payor if the payments are made in the same year as the order or agreement, or in the preceding year, and if the order or agreement specifically provides that the payments will be included in the income of the recipient and will be deductible by the payor.

Payments made directly to third parties may be deductible if the decree, court order, judgement, or written agreement provides that the payments will be treated as income to the recipient and will be deductible to the payor.

Payments to your estranged spouse for specific purposes, and provided for in more recent decrees, written agreements, etc., may also be deductible, depending on the date of your order or agreement and the purpose of the payment. These must be included in your spouse's income as well.

Tax Tip

If you must take legal measures to enforce payment of alimony or maintenance, your legal costs are generally deductible for tax purposes. The legal costs associated with the separation and divorce, however, are not deductible.

You may be able to deduct maintenance payments for your former partner or your children made under a court order on the breakdown of a common-law relationship. Provided that a court order has been issued, the requirements for deductibility by the payor and taxability to the recipient are similar to those discussed for separation or divorce.

Suzanne Thibaudeau v. Her Majesty the Queen

A recent decision of the Federal Court of Appeal has left separated and divorced couples and their advisors flummoxed.

Essentially, the court found that a divorced mother with custody of two minor children does not have to include child support payments from her former husband in her income for tax purposes. The majority decision of the court was that the section of the *Income Tax Act* that requires such amounts to be included in the recipient's income is discriminatory on the basis of family status, i.e., the appellant's status as a separated custodial parent. The decision did not discuss whether support payments should still be tax deductible to the payor, not did it address spousal support payments.

The federal government announced that it will appeal the Thibaudeau decision to the Supreme Court. Of course, an appeal is not automatic: the Supreme Court must grant leave for the appeal. In the meantime, however, the Supreme Court has suspended the effect of the controversial decision.

Revenue Canada issued a release regarding the case: until a decision is made, taxpayers whose circumstances are similar to those covered by the decision and who have filed returns for the 1993 taxation year, have until April 30, 1995 to file a Notice of Objection in order to have their returns reassessed based on the final outcome of the case. Taxpayers in similar circumstances who have not filed 1993 returns should continue to report child support payments as income, pending final outcome of the case. They also have the right to file a Notice of Objection prior to April 30, 1995.

As far as tax returns filed in prior years are concerned, recipients of child support payments may be out of luck once the deadline for filing a Notice of Objection has passed. Taxpayers may request that

Revenue Canada reopen returns going back three years, although Revenue Canada is under no obligation to do so. Even if Revenue Canada agreed to reopen returns, they probably would be held in abeyance until a final decision is made.

Until the matter is settled by the Supreme Court or by Parliament, couples negotiating separation and divorce agreements face uncertainty. Indeed, it would be premature for people to make any changes in the way they view their tax status.

The government could combine the appeal to the Supreme Court with legislative changes, taking the view that the appeal is for past years and that legislation is for the future.

Further, if the legislative change route is taken, it could be retroactive or prospective. Either way, there is the practical matter of how to deal with the huge number of child support arrangements in place that are based on current law. The courts would be tied up for years if even a fraction of such agreements were all re-opened at once.

In reality, recipients of child support payments may find themselves in exactly the same position they were before the Thibaudeau decision. In many separation or divorce agreements, child support payments are grossed-up to take into account the fact that the recipient must pay tax on amounts received. If payors of child support go to court to have the payments reduced to take into account the fact that they are no longer taxable in the recipients' hands, there will be no more dollars to spend on children than there were before the Thibaudeau case.

What do you do about separation agreements currently in place? The decision as it stands today means that many women may net more than they anticipated (at least for the time being). Payors, however, cannot unilaterally cut payments. A payor must get court approval and that is unlikely while the tax situation is still unclear.

Recipients of child support payments may rely on the decision if they so desire, but they should be prepared to deal with a reassessment by Revenue Canada that could be time-consuming and costly if the decision is overturned.

What do you do about separation agreements currently being negotiated? It has been suggested that new agreements be based on the principles in effect before Thibaudeau, with a clause requiring renegotiation or adjustment if the law is ultimately changed. Alternatively, an agreement could be structured to provide for one amount if the decision stands and another if it doesn't. It is unlikely, however, that a judge would find such an agreement acceptable.

At the time of marriage breakdown

Income tax is unlikely to be the prime concern of a couple whose marriage is breaking down. Nevertheless, ignoring the tax consequences can be expensive when negotiating future financial arrangements and the division of property.

Lump sum payments or payments of capital are not deductible. Settlements at the time of divorce cannot be deducted by the payor and do not have to be included in the income of the recipient. While the down payment on a home to be occupied by the spouse is not deductible, payments on account of principal and interest on the mortgage are, up to 20% of the original amount of the debt in any one year, provided the payments and tax consequences are specified in the agreement. The spouse benefitting from these payments has to include this amount in income, but may not receive any cash from the payor with which to satisfy any resulting tax liability.

Attribution rules

Income attribution rules cease to apply upon separation or divorce, as long as the spouses are living apart as a result of their marriage breaking down. However, the spouses must jointly elect for capital gains not to be attributed. This election is intended to prevent one spouse from shouldering the unexpected tax liability that could occur if a capital asset were sold for a sizeable gain, most of which accrued during the marriage.

Capital property transferred to a spouse in settlement of rights that arise out of marriage, or to an individual pursuant to a prescribed court order, will be deemed to be transferred at the adjusted cost base of the property, so that no taxable capital gain will result. However, the transferor may elect otherwise in his or her return for the year of the transfer, and therefore govern the taxation of future capital gains. This should be taken into account in negotiating the settlement.

Personal tax credits

If you are paying alimony or maintenance, in the year of marriage breakdown, you may either claim the married status credit to which you normally would be entitled, or deduct your alimony or maintenance payments. You cannot do both. In either case, the spouse receiving the payments must include them in income.

Tax Tip

Calculate your tax liability using both methods to determine which works out better in your particular situation. Remember that one method involves a deduction, the other a tax credit.

Child Tax Benefit

Under the Child Tax Benefit system, the mother of eligible children ordinarily receives the non-taxable monthly payments. For the purposes of determining the amount of the payments, family earnings and income are combined. On marriage breakdown, the spouse with whom the child or children will be living may elect within 11 months following the month of breakdown that the former spouse's income be ignored for the purposes of computing the child tax benefit for each subsequent month.

Retirement plans

Tax-free transfers of funds from your RRSP or RRIF to your spouse's or common-law spouse's plan(s) are permitted if the transfer is made pursuant to a decree, court order, or judgement or a written separation agreement and the transfer relates to a division of property.

Retirement income payments eventually made will be taxed in the hands of the spouse who is the annuitant under the plan. As well, attribution rules that discourage one spouse from withdrawing the contributions he or she made to a spousal RRSP do not apply in the case of RRSP transfers or withdrawals on the breakdown of a marriage.

Special tax-free transfers are also allowed in the same circumstances from registered pension plans to other RPPs or RRSPs. Often benefits from a plan are split between the spouses, including common-law spouses. Each spouse would receive the appropriate pension payments directly from the plan and be taxable on amounts received.

Canada Pension Plan (CPP) benefits may also be split between estranged spouses. Each spouse would be taxable on the amount received. To avail yourself of this arrangement, you and your spouse must have been legally married and living together for a minimum of 36 consecutive months.

Principal residence

If you and your spouse own only one home at the time of marriage breakdown, the tax-free status of any accrued gain on the family home will generally be maintained. If one spouse continues to live in the home, he or she will be able to designate the home as a principal residence for each of the years it was occupied during the marriage and after the breakdown. The other spouse could acquire a principal residence after the marriage breakdown, and any gain on its disposition would be sheltered by the principal residence exemption.

The situation is more complex where two homes are owned at the time of marriage breakdown. If each home is sold at some point after a divorce, each spouse will want to claim the principal residence exemption for the years during which they were married. However, only one home may be designated by a married couple for years after 1981. One spouse would have to forego designating his or her principal residence for the relevant years of marriage. Alternatively, ownership of one of the houses may be transferred at the time of the marriage breakdown and the available principal residence exemptions used at that time (see page 47).

If two houses eligible for principal residence designation are owned at the time of separation or divorce, careful planning will permit maximum use of the principal residence exemption and the greatest deferral of tax.

The elimination of the $100,000 lifetime capital gains exemption in respect of dispositions of real property purchased after February 1992 meant that all or a portion of a capital gain on the disposition of a family property that is not your principal residence would be subject to tax without the benefit of any sheltering. Draft legislation will implement the 1994 federal budget proposal to eliminate the $100,000 lifetime capital gains exemption altogether for gains realized or accrued after February 22, 1994. There may, however, still be an opportunity for you in 1994 to shelter at least a portion of accrued gains on these types of family properties (see page 104).

⚜ Québec

If you are a separated or divorced person resident in Québec, please note the following Québec differences:

Legal costs

- In addition to the federal rules regarding the deductibility of legal costs, you may be able to deduct (for Québec tax purposes only), the legal or extra-legal expenses you paid, as plaintiff or respondent, for a review of the right to receive or the obligation to pay alimony or a maintenance allowance if certain criteria are met.

  However, the legal or extra-legal expenses paid to establish the initial right to receive or obligation to pay an alimony or maintenance allowance are not deductible.

- The Québec income attribution rules are similar to the federal rules. The introduction by Québec of Bill 146, an Act to amend the Civil Code of Québec, to favour economic equality between the spouses, can create some tax complications on death and marriage breakdown. Professional advice is recommended.

Exclusion of spouse's income after a separation

- Beginning with the 1994 taxation year, a spouse's income after separation will not reduce the married person's tax credit and will not have to be added to the total income used to determine tax benefits such as the income tax reduction for families, the property tax refund, and the refundable tax credit for the QST.

Personal tax credits

In the year of marriage breakdown, Québec generally allows you to claim the married and dependent credits in addition to the alimony payments.

Taxpayers with U.S. Connections

Taxpayers with U.S. Connections

If you are a Canadian resident working, investing, living, or doing business in the U.S, if you own property in the U.S. or if you have or expect to have coverage under U.S. social security, then you may have a U.S. connection for tax purposes. If you are a U.S. citizen with comparable ties to Canada you should review this chapter as well.

Special issues regarding employees on temporary assignment in or from another country are dealt with elsewhere in this book (see page 43).

A Protocol that amends the Canada–U.S. Tax Treaty was signed on August 31, 1994. **Many of the points discussed in this chapter will be affected by the Protocol.** However, until the U.S. Senate approves the Protocol, the dates on which most of its provisions become effective remain uncertain.

This chapter covers pre-Protocol rules. A brief outline of the effect of the Protocol on individual taxpayers is at the end of the chapter.

Canada–U.S. Tax Treaty*

The main purpose of the tax convention between Canada and the United States is to ensure that residents and nationals of the two countries are not subject to double taxation of income. For example, a resident of Canada is taxed on his or her worldwide income. Some of that income may arise in the U.S. and may be subject to U.S. tax as well. The Canadian foreign tax credit rules are designed to ensure that you do not pay Canadian tax on that income, except to the extent that Canadian tax is greater than U.S. tax. The Canada–U.S. Tax Treaty, by excluding all or part of the income from U.S. tax, simplifies the mechanism for protecting against double taxation.

Rules for the taxation of income earned in one jurisdiction by a resident or citizen of another are complex and depend on the nature,

---

* May be affected by the Protocol. See pages 160–161.

and in some cases the magnitude, of income received from U.S. sources, among other things. As a Canadian resident, non-U.S. citizen, you would not ordinarily be required to file a U.S. income tax return if you are receiving interest from deposits in a U.S. bank or if you are receiving dividends from some U.S. shares (such income may, however, be subject to withholding tax at source). On the other hand, if you are providing services in the U.S. in the capacity of an employee, or if you own property in the U.S., you may have to file a U.S. income tax return, even though you may ultimately not have any tax to pay.

Various provisions in the Canada–U.S. Tax Treaty may be significant to you. The table below shows a few types of payments you might be receiving from the U.S. Bear in mind that individual states may not recognize treaty benefits, particularly on employment and pension income.

U.S. Withholding Rates on payments to individuals*

			Percent of payment or proceeds withheld in the U.S. (in general)
Received from the U.S.	Interest		15%
	Dividends		
	Pension payments	Periodic	
		Lump sum	30%
	Capital gain realized by Canadian resident on disposition of U.S. real property*		10%
	Alimony and maintenance		Exempt
	Employment income earned in the U.S.	Within treaty exemption limits**	
		Non-exempt	Applicable federal and state rates

* May apply for withholding certificate. Gain is also subject to tax at applicable federal (and possibly state) rates.

** Exempt by treaty if:
- remuneration is less than U.S. $10,000; or
- the individual was present in the U.S. for less than 184 days and remuneration was not borne by an employer who is a resident of, or has a permanent establishment in, the U.S.

★ May be affected by the Protocol. See pages 160–161.

Tax Tip

Under U.S. domestic law, interest earned on deposits with U.S. banks is generally free of tax when paid to a non-resident. If withholding tax is deducted at source, you should advise the bank immediately. You may have to provide a Certificate of Foreign Status.

Canadian income tax rules are complex enough on their own, without having to take into account the tax rules of another jurisdiction. You should discuss any transborder issues with your professional tax advisor.

Canadian "Snowbirds"*

Many Canadian "Snowbirds" are required to file a special statement with the U.S. tax authorities.

A Canadian citizen and resident will also be considered to be a U.S. resident for tax purposes by the Internal Revenue Service (IRS) if he or she meets a "substantial presence" test. The individual is deemed to meet this test if he or she is present in the U.S. for 31 days during the year and, if pursuant to the following formula, they are present in the U.S. for 183 days or more: ⅙ of the days in the U.S. in the second previous year plus ⅓ of the days in the U.S. in the previous year plus all of the days in the current year. Canadians who spend just over four months per year in the U.S. will generally meet this test.

If an individual is considered to be a resident according to the test above, but spends fewer than 183 days in the U.S. in the current year, has a tax home in a foreign country and a "closer connection" with the foreign country, the individual will not be considered to be a U.S. resident and will not have to file a U.S. resident tax return as long as he or she files a statement with the IRS.

---

* May be affected by the Protocol. See pages 160–161.

A tax home is generally considered to be the country where the individual reports for work or where the individual has his or her regular place of abode. Certain factors are considered in determining whether a "closer connection" exists. These include the location of the individual's permanent home, family, social, and economic ties. The IRS will also consider the location in which the individual holds a driver's licence, voting registration, and country of residence designated on forms and documents.

To claim the "closer connection" exemption, an individual must file Form 8840 or a prescribed statement under penalties of perjury. The statement must contain the following information:

- the individual's name, address, U.S. identification number, and visa number, if any;

- the individual's Canadian passport number;

- the year for which the statement is to apply;

- the number of days of presence in the U.S. during the past three years;

- whether the individual has taken steps to obtain permanent resident status;

- the facts that would indicate a "closer connection" to a foreign country; and

- sufficient evidence to show that the individual has filed a return as a Canadian resident.

The "closer connection" statement must generally be filed by June 15th with the IRS in Philadelphia, Pennsylvania. If a U.S. tax return is otherwise required, the statement should be filed with the return. Failure to file the statement could result in the individual's being treated as a U.S. resident subject to U.S. tax.

Apart from the Canada–U.S. tax treaty, a Canadian resident who does not meet the "closer connection" test, (i.e., who has a U.S. "green card" (permanent residence status) or who spends 183 or more days in the U.S. in a year) will be considered to be a U.S. resident for tax purposes and required to file a U.S. tax return. However, such an individual would probably be considered a resident of Canada under the treaty. As a resident of Canada, the individual will generally be able to exclude non-U.S. income from the U.S. return. The individual will, however, be required to file a treaty-based disclosure form (see below) and disclose his or her world income.

In view of the serious implications, you should consult your professional tax advisor if you regularly spend time in the U.S. or if you have a vacation or retirement home there.

Disclosure of treaty-based filing positions*

Canadian individuals who benefit from the Canada–U.S. tax treaty may have to file a statement disclosing the fact that a treaty provision has been used to reduce or eliminate U.S. tax that would otherwise be payable. In cases in which no U.S. tax return is filed, a disclosure statement may still have to be filed if a taxpayer relies on a treaty-based benefit.

The reporting requirement is waived when the return-based position pertains to, among other things:

- treaty-reduced withholding payments such as interest, dividends, rents, or royalties paid to unrelated parties; and

- a reduction or modification of taxation of income derived from wages and salaries, pensions, annuities, and social security payments.

However, other situations will require disclosure. For example, if a Canadian resident does not meet the "closer connection" test (see "Canadian Snowbirds" above) and is relying on the Canada–U.S. treaty to exclude non-U.S. income from a U.S. return, disclosure

---

* May be affected by the Protocol. See pages 160–161.

will generally be required. When a Canadian relies on a provision of the Canada–U.S. treaty that reduces or modifies the taxation of a gain or loss from the disposition of U.S. real property interests, or claims application of the non-discrimination clause of the treaty, disclosure will also generally be required.

Although it is not an official form, IRS form 8833 may be used to provide the necessary information. The form, or other similar disclosure statement, should be filed with an individual's tax return. Fairly detailed information must be reported, including the taxpayer's name and address, the nature and amount of the gross receipts on which the treaty benefit is claimed, and a statement of facts relied upon to support each separate position taken.

Penalties for failure to disclose a treaty-based position are stiff. For an individual, the fine is $1,000 per position not disclosed.

Canada–U.S. Social Security Agreement*

The reciprocal Social Security Agreement between Canada and the United States coordinates the social security programs that provide old age, disability, survivor, and death benefits of the two countries. It protects the social security rights that Canadian and U.S. migrant workers have earned through a combination of residence status and social insurance contributions. It also provides for continuity of coverage and ensures that a worker will not be contributing to both countries' social security schemes for the same work.

If you receive retirement or survivor benefits under the *U.S. Social Security Act,* only one-half of the amount need be included in your income for Canadian income tax purposes. The first $1,000 is also eligible for the pension income tax credit. Moreover, as long as you are not a U.S. citizen, the benefits are not subject to U.S. tax.

---

* May be affected by the Protocol. See pages 160–161.

158 | U.S. estate tax*

U.S. federal estate tax rates for non-residents ranging from 18 to 55% may create significant estate tax liabilities for Canadians who die owning U.S. "situs property" having a net realizable value in excess of U.S. $60,000. U.S. situs property includes: real estate (a vacation condominium, a private house, or U.S. real estate used or held in connection with a U.S. business venture); shares of a U.S. corporation (whether public or private); debt obligations issued by U.S. residents (including debt obligations issued by the U.S. government); and other personal property situated in the U.S. (including furnishings, cars, boats, jewellery, and even the value of a membership in a U.S. club).

The U.S. estate tax is levied on the fair market value of property owned by the deceased as of the date of death. Non-recourse debt attributable to U.S. assets, as well as a portion of other liabilities, may be deducted to arrive at the net taxable value of an estate.

Canada has no estate tax. Instead, Canadian income tax law deems a disposition of the decedent's property on death and income tax is levied on the accrued capital gains. Canadian income tax on accrued gains on property that passes from the decedent to the surviving spouse or to a spousal trust can be deferred until the death of the surviving spouse. The opportunity for a Canadian to defer U.S. estate tax until the death of a surviving spouse is more limited. In fact, property bequeathed by an individual to a surviving spouse may be subject to U.S. estate tax twice – once on the death of the individual and again on the death of the spouse.

Canadians who die owning property subject to U.S. estate tax may also be faced with Canadian capital gains tax as a result of the deemed disposition on death rules. There is no relief by way of foreign tax credit for U.S. estate tax payable and no tax treaty protection to eliminate double taxation. (Discussions between the Department of Finance of Canada and the Treasury Department of the United States

---

* May be affected by the Protocol. See pages 160–161.

with respect to income and estate tax matters that began in 1990 are continuing. Apparently, the discussions are focusing primarily on the effect of the U.S. federal estate tax and the effects on nationals of both countries of the Canada–U.S. Income Tax Convention.)

Deposits with U.S. banks or savings and loan associations, as well as proceeds from life insurance policies, are excluded from the U.S. taxable estate of a non-resident, non-citizen decedent.

Tax Tip

Consider the following suggestions for reducing your U.S. taxable estate:

- Split property with your spouse and/or among your children. Every individual is entitled to his or her own estate tax credit.

- Refinance — non-recourse loans secured by U.S. situs property reduce the net taxable value of an estate.

- Rent rather than buy personal use property, such as cars, boats, and vacation properties.

- Change your investment portfolio and reinvest in Canada or elsewhere.

- Consider the use of a Canadian corporation to hold your U.S. property.

- Evaluate the cost of life insurance as a means of funding a possible U.S. tax liability.

Professional tax advice is a must before you attempt to implement any strategy to reduce or eliminate your exposure to U.S. estate tax.

160 ⚜ Québec

If you are a Québec resident with a U.S. connection for tax purposes, or if you are a U.S. citizen with comparable ties with Québec, the federal rules generally apply with the following difference.

Québec–U.S. Social Security Agreement

Since Québec has its own social security program, which provides pension, disability, survivor, and death benefits through the Québec Pension Plan, it has entered into its own U.S. Social Security Agreement. The agreement is similar to the one entered into by Canada.

If you receive retirement or survivor benefits under the U.S. Social Security Act, only one-half of the amount need be included in your income for Québec income tax purposes.* The first $1,000 is also eligible for the pension income tax credit.

The Tax Protocol's effect on individuals

Effective Dates

The Protocol will come into effect when it is approved by the U.S. Senate, which is unlikely to be before mid-1995. Provisions affecting U.S. federal estate taxes will be retroactive to November 10, 1988. Withholding tax rates will become effective at the beginning of the second month after the month in which the U.S. Senate gives its approval. Other provisions will become effective on the January 1st after the U.S. Senate gives its approval (i.e., most likely January 1, 1996, but possibly not until January 1, 1997).

---

* May be affected by the Protocol. See pages 160–161.

Withholding Tax Rates

The withholding tax rate on cross-border interest payments will drop from 15% to 10%. On dividends, for most individuals the rate will stay at 15%. Royalties and rents remain subject to a 10% withholding tax rate, except for certain payments in respect of the use of technology, which become exempt from withholding tax.

Relief from U.S. Federal Estate Taxes

The Protocol provides a possible exemption for a smaller estate and some tax credit relief for a larger estate. However, Canadians with real property interests in the U.S. or significant U.S. investments should still review their portfolio arrangements with a view to taking advantage of U.S. estate tax planning techniques.

The Protocol establishes a new threshold value for estates in respect of deaths after November 10, 1988. If the value of the worldwide gross estate of a Canadian resident does not exceed US$1.2 million, the estate will be subject to federal U.S. estate taxes only in respect of property whose sale would yield a gain that would be taxable to an individual as a result of the provisions in the Treaty that deal with gains. In effect, real property, resource property and business property of a permanent establishment may become subject to U.S. federal estate tax.

In addition, a Canadian resident will generally be treated no less favourably than a U.S. citizen with respect to U.S. estate taxes. A Canadian will be entitled to two credits against the estate tax: a marital property credit (of up to US$192,800) for spousal bequests of U.S.–situated property and the so-called "unified credit" (also up to US$192,800).

Any U.S. estate taxes that are paid will be recognized for credit against Canadian income taxes imposed on U.S. source income arising in the year of death.

Amending previously filed U.S. estate tax returns and Canadian income tax returns for the year of death could yield significant tax savings, because the new rules will apply retroactively. Claims for refunds must be filed by the later of one year after the date on which the Protocol enters into force and the end of the statutory period otherwise prescribed by domestic law.

Social Security Payments

Canadian-resident beneficiaries of U.S. retirement arrangements and U.S.-resident beneficiaries of Canadian retirement arrangements will be allowed to elect to defer Canadian or U.S. taxation, respectively, until funds are received from the plans. Social security payments will be taxed only in the country that makes the payments.

Gambling

The Protocol permits Canadian residents who gamble in the U.S. to offset gains with losses resulting from wagering transactions, for the purpose of computing their U.S. tax liability.

Calculating Your Taxes

Calculating Your Taxes

Ultimately your tax has to be calculated – first by you or your advisor, then by Revenue Canada. Even after all the elements in your tax return are determined, calculating your tax can be a confusing exercise, even when you are using the tax tables provided in the Revenue Canada Guide, or a commercial computer program.

This chapter, along with information that Revenue Canada provides, will help guide you through the many steps involved in calculating your tax. Throughout the chapter you will encounter references to the personal tax flowchart (developed especially for this book to show how the various elements in a tax calculation are related). The flowchart appears twice (pages 167 and 177). The second version has an extra section that deals with alternative minimum tax (AMT). (The chapter, however, will still make sense even if you prefer to ignore the flowcharts.)

As in other chapters, material at the end highlights important additional information and differences for Québec taxpayers.

Taxable income

Total income

Your total income is the aggregate of income from employment, investments, taxable capital gains, pensions, and business income [flowchart box 1]. These have been discussed in other chapters of this book.

After working out your total income, you calculate your taxable income in two stages: your total income less certain deductions and adjustments equals net income; and net income less other deductions gives you your taxable income.

Deductions

The first set of deductions includes RRSP and RPP contributions, union or professional dues, child care expenses, ABILs, moving expenses, alimony or maintenance payments, and interest and carrying charges for investments [flowchart box 2]. Another important deduction in arriving at net income is the social benefits repayment ("clawback") discussed later in this chapter [flowchart box 14].

Subtracting these deductions from your total income yields your net income [flowchart box 3]. Net income is used in a number of preliminary calculations, such as the "equivalent-to-married" credit.

A second set of deductions [flowchart box 4] includes the capital gains deduction (if applicable), the employee home relocation deduction, stock option and share deductions, and deductions for net capital and noncapital losses from previous years.

Subtracting this second set of deductions from net income produces your taxable income [flowchart box 5].

Taxable income and net income are used in some provinces' surtax calculations (see Appendix 5).

Federal tax

Federal tax is calculated using your taxable income and the federal marginal rates [flowchart boxes 5 and 6] found in Appendix 4 (or in Schedule 1 of your 1994 return). Once you have determined your federal tax, you will have to subtract some tax credits and add the federal surtax. As well, you will have to make a number of other adjustments and calculate provincial (or territorial) income tax before arriving at your actual tax liability for the year.

If your return is straightforward and your taxable income is $59,180 or less, you may be able to use Tax Tables A and B (provided in the government's Tax Return Guide) to compute federal income tax and surtax, and provincial tax.

| ## Non-refundable personal, dividend, and other tax credits

From the amount you have calculated, you deduct your personal and other non-refundable tax credits [flowchart box 8] (including self-employed CPP contributions [flowchart box 13]). These credits are based on amounts you claim. Every taxpayer claims the basic personal amount; other claims depend on individual circumstances: Are you married? Are you age 65 or over? Did you have substantial medical expenses? Did you make any charitable donations?

Your credit is calculated as 17% of the total of these claims (except that higher charitable donations are credited at 29%).

Sufficient credits could reduce your basic federal tax [flowchart box 9] to zero, eliminating your federal and provincial income tax liabilities. They cannot produce a negative amount that would create a refund, unlike some other credits (which are refundable) discussed later.

Appendix 6 sets out the various personal tax credits.

• Personal tax credits

Personal tax credits [flowchart boxes 8 and 10] are the first non-refundable tax credits. They reduce your federal tax. Personal tax credits are equal to 17% of your "claim amounts". For example, as noted above, everyone is entitled to claim the basic personal amount, which is $6,456 for 1994. At 17%, the claim translates into a credit of $1,098.

If you are married, you may claim an amount in respect of a spouse you are supporting. The claim, and hence the credit, will be reduced dollar for dollar if your spouse's net income is over $538, dropping to zero at a net income of $5,918.

You may claim an equivalent-to-married credit if you are single, widowed, separated, or divorced and you wholly support a person related to you by blood, marriage, or adoption. Except in the case of a dependent child, the person you are supporting must reside with you in Canada. The person you support must be under 18 years of

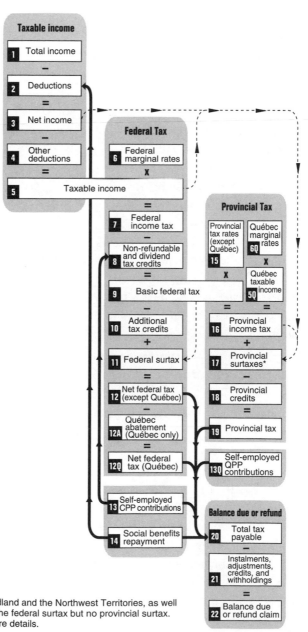

* Residents of Newfoundland and the Northwest Territories, as well
as non-residents, pay the federal surtax but no provincial surtax.
See Appendix 5 for more details.

age, unless that person is your parent or grandparent, or unless the person was dependent on you because of a mental or physical infirmity. The amount of the equivalent-to-married credit is the same as the married credit. Further, only one equivalent-to-married credit may be claimed per household.

While you may claim only one equivalent-to-married credit, you may also claim credits for dependents (you or your spouse's children, grandchildren, parents, grandparents, brothers, sisters, aunts, uncles, nieces and nephews, and in-laws, too) who are totally dependent on you for support. The dependents must be 18 years of age or older and must be physically or mentally handicapped. The claim amount is $1,583 if the dependent's net income is less than $2,690, dropping to nil at a net income of $4,273.

The credit for dependent children under 18 years of age was eliminated, effective January 1, 1993. Family allowances, the credit for dependent children and the refundable child tax credit were replaced with the Child Tax Benefit system. Refer to page 180 for further details.

If you are disabled, a disability tax credit is available. Generally, your daily living activities must be markedly restricted and the impairment must have lasted or be expected to last for a continuous period of at least 12 months. A doctor must certify the disability on a prescribed form, the Disability Tax Credit Certificate, which must be filed with your return when you first make your claim. The disability tax credit for 1994 is $720.

A taxpayer may also claim the unused part of a dependent's disability credit. You may claim the credit for a person in respect of whom you claimed the equivalent-to-married credit, or for a dependent child or grandchild who is 18 years of age or over and who has a mental or physical handicap.

Certain non-refundable credits that your spouse does not require to reduce tax payments to zero may be transferred to you. The age, disability, tuition and education fees, and pension income credits are all transferable.

• UI, CPP or QPP credits

If you paid unemployment insurance (UI) premiums or contributed to the CPP or QPP, you are entitled to credits based on your contributions and the maximum required.

• Pension income credit

If you receive various types of pension income, you are entitled to a pension income credit of 17% of eligible pension income, to a maximum credit of $170 (or $1,000 of pension income). The credit is transferable to your spouse to the extent that you are unable to use it (see page 134 for the types of pension income that are eligible for the credit and strategies to ensure that you will be entitled to use it).

• Age credit

You are entitled to claim an age credit if you are age 65 or over. The federal age credit is $592 in 1994, which is 17% of the "age amount" of $3,482.

The federal budget proposes that the age credit be subject to an income test. The age amount will be reduced by 7.5% of your net income exceeding $25,921 in 1994 and by 15% in subsequent years. The reduction is to be phased in over two years. In 1994 the reduction stops when the age amount (and hence the credit) is cut in half. After that, the reduction continues until the age amount and the credit disappear. Accordingly, if your income is over $49,134, you will lose one half of the age credit in 1994 and will not be able to claim the age credit at all in 1995 and subsequent taxation years.

The age amount will not be reduced if the credit is transferred from your spouse.

• Tuition and education tax credits

The federal tuition credit is 17% of eligible tuition fees to the extent that the fees exceed $100. The education credit is 17% of $80, for each month or part of a month that the student was enrolled in a qualifying educational program as a full-time student at a designated

170 educational institution. The student need only be enrolled in a qualifying program; he or she need not be actually attending the designated educational institution. This ensures that the credit is available to students participating in distance education programs or correspondence courses. Entitlement to both credits must be supported by Form T2202 or Form T2202A, which the educational institution will provide. Enrollment in either a Canadian or foreign educational institution may entitle the student to a credit.

Tax Tip

The tax credits may be transferable from the student to a supporting person, generally a parent, grandparent, or spouse. Only the amount that the student is unable to use to reduce his or her federal tax to zero can be transferred. The total of tuition and education credits that can be transferred is limited to $680.

Tuition fees may be claimed only on a calendar year basis. On your 1994 return, for example, you may only claim fees paid for courses taken between January 1 and December 31, 1994.

• Medical expense tax credit

You may claim a tax credit for medical expenses paid within any 12-month period ending in the year. Expenses for which you are reimbursed, either by your employer or a private or government-sponsored health care plan, are not eligible for the credit. However, few plans reimburse 100% of expenses, and the difference between the amount you actually pay and the amount received from the health plan is a medical expense.

The list of eligible medical expenses is extensive and includes fees paid to a private health or dental plan. While most of us are pretty good about keeping our receipts for doctor, dentist, and pharmacy bills, we tend to forget about receipts for premiums paid to private plans. Make sure that you and your spouse (and other family members where appropriate) keep them. The receipts must be attached to your tax returns to be eligible for the credit.

Total eligible medical expenses must first be reduced by the lesser of 3% of your net income and $1,614 in 1994. This amount is indexed annually in the same way as personal tax credits. The $1,614 cap takes effect if your net income is over $53,800. The tax credit is 17% of the amount remaining.

Tax Tip

Carefully select the 12-month period for medical expenses. Keep your receipts for 1995 if some 1994 expenses are not claimed on your 1994 return.

Up to $5,000 of part-time attendant care expenses that are not otherwise deductible in computing income qualify for the medical expense tax credit. Eligible expenses are those incurred by or on behalf of a disabled person who qualifies for the disability tax credit in respect of an attendant who is not related to the disabled person.

Also eligible for the medical expense tax credit is the cost of:

- specially trained service animals that assist individuals with severe and prolonged impairment that restricts the use of their arms and legs;

- modifications to the home to enable a person with a severe and permanent mobility restriction to gain access to the home or rooms in it; and

- incontinence products required by reason of a physical impairment.

The list of eligible medical expenses for the purposes of the medical expense tax credit also includes the cost of visual or vibratory signalling devices to those with a hearing impairment and expenses for rehabilitative therapy to adjust for speech or hearing loss, including training in lip reading and sign language.

Charitable donation tax credit

Donations made to registered Canadian charities are eligible for a tax credit on your income tax return. While the amount of donations that may be claimed in any one year is limited to 20% of your net income, donations in excess of the limit may be carried forward for five years. More generous rules deal with qualifying donations to the Crown or donations of certified Canadian cultural property. Donations to specified foreign universities are also eligible for the credit. Donations to other U.S. charities or foreign charities in countries with which Canada has a tax treaty are also eligible, but generally only to the extent that you have income from the foreign jurisdiction. The 20% limitation also applies in the case of foreign donations.

You must file official tax receipts with your tax return. (Cancelled cheques are not acceptable.) Otherwise, the tax credit may be disallowed.

The tax credit for charitable donations is two-tiered. The credit is 17% of the first $200 of charitable donations plus 29% on any excess. (For 1994 and subsequent taxation years, the federal budget proposes to lower the threshold for the higher credit slightly from $250 to $200). Either spouse may claim the donations of the other, no matter whose name is on the official receipt.

Tax Tip

If you and your spouse donate over $200 in any one year, the tax credit will be larger if one spouse claims the entire amount. For example, if you and your spouse each donates $200 and claim a tax credit on your own returns for the donations made, your tax credit would be $34.50 each ($200 × 17%), for a family total of $68. On the other hand, if one of you included the entire amount of donations on your return, the tax credit would be $92 (200 × 17% + $200 × 29%).

Remember that tax advantages are an added benefit of charitable giving; as with your investment decisions, tax is only one factor.

A donation that offers little or no tax benefit should not be rejected on that ground alone.

Tax Tip
Watch the timing of your donations. If you donate $400 this year, $200 of your tax credit will be calculated at 17% and $200 at 29%. If, instead, you donate $200 in December and another $200 in January of the following year, your tax credit will be determined using 17% in both years, and your tax credit will be $24 less.

• Dividend tax credit
In addition to deducting non-refundable tax credits from federal tax on taxable income, you are also entitled to a dividend tax credit if you reported dividends from taxable Canadian corporations [flowchart box 8]. On your tax return, the actual amount of your dividend is grossed up by 25%. The dividend tax credit is 13⅓% of this grossed-up or taxable amount of dividends that you reported (see also page 82).

If you paid alternative minimum tax (AMT, described below), in prior years, you may be able to credit the payment and to reduce your tax.

At this point, the amount of basic federal tax [flowchart box 9] is preserved for computing provincial income taxes and the federal surtax, and for comparison with AMT. However, further adjustments enter into the calculation of federal income tax.

The remaining steps in your tax calculation are the same whether you have to pay AMT or not. The only differences are that if you have to pay AMT:

- the basic federal tax [flowchart box 9] is replaced by the "minimum amount" from the AMT calculation; and

- the additional tax credits [flowchart box 10] are replaced by a special foreign tax credit.

Additional tax credits

🌐 Foreign tax credit

You may reduce tax payable by claiming a non-refundable tax credit for income or profits taxes paid to a foreign government [flowchart box 10]. The credit is equal to the lesser of the foreign tax paid and Canadian tax payable on that income. A separate calculation must be made for each foreign country. A separate calculation is also required for business income taxes and non-business income taxes paid to each foreign country. Unusable foreign business income tax credits may be carried back three years and forward seven. Non-business income taxes do not enjoy the same treatment; however, to the extent that foreign tax on your investment income exceeds 15% of the foreign income, the excess is deductible in computing income subject to tax.

You may also be able to claim a provincial foreign tax credit to the extent that you were unable to claim the entire foreign tax credit on your federal return.

• Political contribution tax credit

You may claim a tax credit on your federal income tax return for contributions made to federal political parties [flowchart box 10]. Official receipts must be filed with your return. Most provinces have similar credits for political contributions to provincial parties.

The credit is calculated as follows: 75% of the first $100; 50% on the next $450 and 33⅓% of any contributions over $550. The maximum credit allowed in any one year is $500, which means that you get no credit for political contributions in excess of $1,150.

Tax Tip

Consider spreading your political contributions out over two years. For example, if you contribute $700 in 1994, your federal tax credit will be $350. If instead you contribute $350 in 1994 and $350 in the following year, your tax credits will be $200 each year, a $50 increase.

Federal surtax

The federal individual surtax [flowchart box 11] has two levels, both based on basic federal tax.

The first level applies to everyone: it is 3% of basic federal tax.

The second, the "high-earner" surtax, is determined as 5% of any basic federal tax over $12,500. A taxpayer resident in Canada with the fewest and smallest possible credits and no deductions will begin paying the second-tier surtax after earning approximately $62,195. At that level the federal marginal rate is 29%, so at 8% of basic federal tax the federal surtax adds 2.32% to the marginal rate. For more on the calculation of the federal surtax, see Appendix 4.

The total federal surtax is added to the federal component of your income tax.

Provincial, territorial, and non-resident taxes

Provincial, territorial, and non-resident taxes provide a tier of income tax that adds roughly 45 to 69% to your tax bill [flowchart boxes 15 to 19], before any provincial surtaxes are added. Except for Québec, provincial taxes are determined by applying the appropriate provincial rate to basic federal tax (see Appendix 5). In addition, most provinces have their own systems of surtaxes and tax reductions (see Appendix 5). Outside Québec you do not file a separate provincial tax return; rather, you calculate the provincial tax owing and remit it, along with your federal income tax return and federal balance payable to Ottawa, where it is allocated to the appropriate province.

Québec's tax system is more complex. Rather than calculating tax as a percentage of the federal level, Québec has a parallel system that closely resembles the federal one, but requires a separate return and payments directly to the provincial government [flowchart boxes 5Q to 16]. Refer to the Québec section on page 77 for further details about that province's tax regime.

If you are filing a Québec income tax return, your federal return will also be affected. In recognition of the fact that Québec collects its own taxes, a refundable Québec abatement, simply a credit of 16.5% based on your basic federal tax [flowchart box 12A], is deductible in calculating your net federal tax [flowchart box 12Q].

The Yukon and Northwest Territories also impose taxes comparable to provinces other than Québec.

A Canadian resident individual typically pays provincial tax to the province or territory of which he or she is a resident on December 31. Non-residents of Canada who receive income from Canadian sources (for example, rental income, pensions, annuities, alimony, and capital gains) may be subject to federal tax. While non-residents will not ordinarily be subject to provincial income tax because they are not resident in a province or territory, they may be subject to a federal surtax that applies to income earned outside a province. This surtax has the effect of putting a non-resident in a position comparable to that faced by a resident. Of course, non-residents earning Canadian source employment or business income may have to pay provincial or territorial tax on such income.

Social benefit repayment ("clawback")

If you received unemployment insurance (UI) or OAS benefits, you may have to repay a portion, depending on your income. If your net income exceeded $58,110, you must repay a portion of the UI

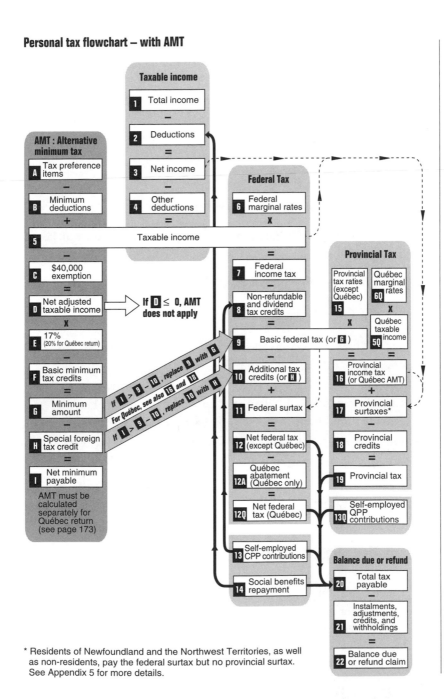

Taxable income

1 Total income
−
2 Deductions
=
3 Net income
−
4 Other deductions
=

5 Taxable income

AMT : Alternative minimum tax

A Tax preference items
−
B Minimum deductions
+

−
C $40,000 exemption
−
D Net adjusted taxable income
X
E 17% (20% for Québec return)
−
F Basic minimum tax credits
=
G Minimum amount
−
H Special foreign tax credit
=
I Net minimum payable

AMT must be calculated separately for Québec return (see page 173)

If **D** ≤ 0, AMT does not apply

If **I** > **9** – **10** , replace **9** with **G**
For Québec, see also **16** and **13**
If **I** > **9** – **10** , replace **10** with **H**

Federal Tax

6 Federal marginal rates
X
=
7 Federal income tax
−
8 Non-refundable and dividend tax credits
=
9 Basic federal tax (or **G**)
−
10 Additional tax credits (or **H**)
+
11 Federal surtax
=
12 Net federal tax (except Québec)
−
12A Québec abatement (Québec only)
=
12Q Net federal tax (Québec)

13 Self-employed CPP contributions

14 Social benefits repayment

Provincial Tax

15 Provincial tax rates (except Québec)
6Q Québec marginal rates
X
X
5Q Québec taxable income
=
=
16 Provincial income tax (or Québec AMT)
+
17 Provincial surtaxes*
=
18 Provincial credits
=
19 Provincial tax

13Q Self-employed QPP contributions

Balance due or refund

20 Total tax payable

21 Instalments, adjustments, credits, and withholdings

22 Balance due or refund claim

* Residents of Newfoundland and the Northwest Territories, as well as non-residents, pay the federal surtax but no provincial surtax. See Appendix 5 for more details.

178

benefits you received [flowchart box 14]. That payment is deductible [flowchart box 2]. The calculation for OAS is outlined elsewhere in this book (see page 135).

Balance due or refund claimed

To calculate your total tax payable [flowchart box 20], add:

• the net federal tax [flowchart box 12];

• any self-employed CPP contributions you are required to make [flowchart box 13];

• the "clawback" [flowchart box 14]; and

• total provincial tax [flowchart box 19].

Only a few more items [flowchart box 21] need to be considered before the tax calculation is complete.

You subtract any tax you have already paid, particularly amounts that have been withheld at source, any instalments of tax that you have made throughout the year, and overpayments of CPP or UI premiums. The refundable tax credits, including the investment tax credit and any provincial tax credits are also subtracted [flowchart box 21].

At last you know how much you owe Revenue Canada, or how much Revenue Canada owes you as a refund [flowchart box 22].

Alternative minimum tax (AMT)

If your calculation of taxable income [flowchart box 5] reflects "tax preference items" [flowchart box A★] that lower your tax bill, you should calculate your net adjusted taxable income [flowchart box D★]

★ Refer to Personal Tax flowchart with AMT, page 177.

and your minimum amount [flowchart box G★] to determine if you are liable for alternative minimum tax (AMT).

Tax preference items to be included in adjusted taxable income for this calculation include certain deductions, and income that is subject to special rules. The most common tax preference items are:

- contributions to RPPs, RRSPs, DPSPs (less lump-sum receipts);

- CCA claimed on MURBs and certified film properties (less income before CCA);

- resource expenditures, depletion and resource allowances (less resource income); and

- the non-taxable portion of capital gains.

A non-arm's length sale to realize capital gains may result in a minimum tax liability.

Your minimum amount [flowchart box G★] is calculated by applying a federal rate of 17% [flowchart box E★] to net adjusted taxable income [flowchart box D★]. If your net adjusted taxable income is zero or less, you need not go any further: AMT does not apply to you. While no refundable credits or dividend tax credits are available (although the dividend gross-up is excluded from income), you may deduct basic minimum tax credits [flowchart box F★] to arrive at your minimum amount [flowchart box G★].

You should not have to pay AMT unless your tax preference items exceed the $40,000 exemption [flowchart box C★]. Even then the 17% rate may be lower than your "regular" tax rate, which means you won't be subject to AMT.

From your minimum amount, you may deduct a special foreign tax credit [flowchart box H★], leaving you with your net minimum payable [flowchart box I★]. The special foreign tax credit is similar to the regular foreign tax credit, discussed above.

★ Refer to Personal Tax flowchart with AMT, page 177.

Your net minimum payable [flowchart box I★] is compared to your basic federal tax less additional tax credits [flowchart box 9 less box 10] and the larger amount is used in subsequent tax calculations. Accordingly, if you are liable for AMT, your federal surtax and provincial tax will increase.

AMT is a complex calculation, and there are other more unusual elements to consider. Revenue Canada has provided Form T691 for calculating AMT. You are even better off if you use one of the available computer programs for preparing your return; the calculation will be done automatically.

If you are required to pay AMT, you are entitled to a credit in future years when your basic federal tax [flowchart box 9] exceeds your AMT minimum amount [flowchart box G★] for that year. The credit is the excess of AMT over your regular liability. The carryforward period is seven years, and the credit each year cannot reduce your liability below your AMT amount for that year.

Child Tax Benefit system

The Child Tax Benefit system replaced the system of family allowances, non-refundable child tax credits for children under age 18 and the refundable child tax credit. This system provides the same level of benefit per child to families in similar financial circumstances.

What are the particulars? The Child Tax Benefit is paid monthly, generally to the mother. The benefit is calculated by the government on the basis of tax information from the previous year. The basic benefit of $1,020 per child may be supplemented by:

- $75 for the third and each subsequent child in a family; and

- $213 per child under age seven when no child care expenses are claimed.

★ Refer to Personal Tax flowchart with AMT, page 177.

Low-income working families with children also receive an earned-income supplement of up to $500 per family. The supplement is reduced when family adjusted income exceeds $20,921.

The Child Tax Benefit does not have to be included in your income nor is it recovered on your tax return. The amount of the benefit is, however, reduced by a factor based on net family income and the number of children in the family. In particular, the benefit is reduced by 2.5% of family income in excess of $25,921 for families with one child and 5% of the same amount for families with more than one child.

⚜ Québec

Québec residents do not calculate their provincial taxes as a percentage of federal tax (see Appendix 2). Instead, Québec has a parallel tax regime that closely resembles the federal system and requires a separate provincial return in addition to the one you file for federal purposes. The calculation of Québec taxable income is slightly different [flowchart box 5Q] as are the marginal rates that are applied to Québec taxable income [flowchart box 6Q] to determine your Québec tax liability.

If you pay your federal tax by instalments, you may have to remit instalments of tax to Québec as well (see page 190).

Credits and deductions

While most of the federal tax credits [flowchart box 8] are available in Québec, the amounts and types of credits differ somewhat.

182 | ## Changes in the determination of net income

- Tuition fees are considered to be deductions in the determination of net income in Québec, whereas they are a non-refundable tax credit for federal tax purposes.

- Child care expenses have become refundable tax credits in Québec, although they remain a deduction in determining income for federal tax purposes.

Non-refundable tax credits

• Amount for a person living alone

A credit of $1,050 may be claimed in Québec by a person living alone and who:

- during all of 1994, maintained a self-contained domestic establishment in which no other person lived during the year, with the exception of a person for whom an amount for dependent children could be claimed;

- was not married at any time in 1994 or, if married, was not supporting his or her spouse; and

- did not have a common-law spouse at any time in 1994 or, if he or she did, was not supporting the common-law spouse.

    The fact that a person made alimony payments entitling him or her to a deduction does not in itself mean that the person is considered to have been supporting a spouse or common-law spouse.

    This amount may not be claimed in the income tax return of a deceased person.

• Married person tax credit

Beginning with the 1994 taxation year, a spouse's income after separation will not reduce the married person's tax credit and will not have to be added to the total income used to determine tax benefits such as the income tax reduction for families, the property tax refund and the refundable tax credit for the QST.

• Tax credit for dependent children
The amount of the tax credit for a second and each subsequent child has been increased from $2,250 to $2,400 for 1994.

• Tax credit for the elderly
At present, taxpayers aged 65 or over are entitled, for Québec income tax purposes, to a nonrefundable tax credit equal to 20% of $2,200, representing a reduction of up to $440 in the amount of income tax they have to pay. Under the federal tax system, taxpayers aged 65 or over are also entitled to a non-refundable tax credit. However, since the federal budget of February 22, 1994, this federal old age tax credit is subject to an income test as of 1995. The Québec tax system will not be harmonized with this federal measure.

Refundable tax credits

• Tax credit for elderly persons housed by others
Québec grants a refundable tax credit to persons who lodge the elderly. The amount on which this tax credit is based has been increased from $2,200 to $2,750, raising the credit from $440 to $550 for each adult lodged in 1994. To be eligible for this tax credit, the housed parent must be aged 70 or over, or 60 or over and suffering from a prolonged, severe mental or physical disability.

• Tax credit for employees of the elderly
The 1994 Québec budget introduced a new refundable tax credit for persons aged 65 or over who incur costs by hiring persons to do domestic work. The credit is equal to 30% of any salaries paid to such persons, up to a maximum of $10,000 (for a maximum credit

184 of $3,000). This credit will be reduced as family income increases, by 10% for every dollar of income in excess of $30,000 in total family income.

To ease the administrative burden associated with determining source deductions and payments to be made for these domestic employees, the government of Québec has proposed paying payroll taxes on behalf of taxpayers. It will be necessary to conclude an agreement with the federal government with regard to federal income tax and unemployment insurance contributions. In addition, any form of government assistance received in respect of eligible expenses for purposes of the tax credit will have to be subtracted from the eligible expenses.

• Tax credit for adoption expenses

The 1994 Québec budget introduced a new refundable tax credit for adoption expenses, to apply as of 1994. This credit will be equal to 20% of eligible adoption expenses incurred for a child and paid by the individual or by his or her spouse. It may not exceed $1,000 per child (for a maximum of $5,000 in eligible expenses). This measure applies to final adoption orders handed down after December 31, 1993. A copy of the final adoption order or proof of its registration at the Court of Québec, as the case may be, will have to be forwarded with the income tax return of the taxpayer claiming the tax credit.

Other measures

• The 1994 Québec budget introduced the possibility, for a municipality, of deferring payment of property taxes payable by an elderly person. If you are a property owner aged 65 or over and are unable to pay your property taxes, contact your municipality, which may be able to help you.

If you are self-employed in Québec, you will need to add self-employed Québec Pension Plan (QPP) premiums to your Québec

tax liability [flowchart box 13Q] and remit this amount to the
province, instead of remitting self-employed CPP premiums to the
federal government as you would in the case of the other provinces
and territories [flowchart box 13]. The premiums under both QPP
and CPP are the same.

Health services fund contribution

The health services fund contribution is discussed under that heading
in the Employees chapter on page 54.

Alternative minimum tax (AMT)

The Québec AMT is calculated at a rate of 20% [flowchart box E⋆].
The adjusted taxable income [flowchart box D⋆] on which Québec
AMT is calculated can also be different, because net income for
Québec tax purposes may be different from federal net income.

To ensure that high-income taxpayers are required to contribute
to the financing of public expenditures on the basis of their ability
to pay, the strategic investments for the Québec economy account
has been eliminated as of the 1994 taxation year. Thus, a taxpayer
who formerly benefited from preferential tax treatment in Québec
will have to include all of his or her strategic investments when
determining whether or not he or she is subject to the alternative
minimum tax. However, individual deductions included in this
account will continue to be eligible deductions in the determination
of a taxpayer's taxable income.

⋆ Refer to Personal Tax flowchart with AMT, page 177.

Québec surtaxes

In Québec, a surtax equal to 5% of the provincial tax that exceeds $5,000 and another 5% of the tax that exceeds $10,000 must be added.

However, in its 1994 budget, Québec introduced a tax reduction applicable as of the 1994 taxation year equal to 2% of the excess of $10,000 over tax payable after deducting non-refundable tax credits.

Filing Returns and Paying Your Taxes

Filing Returns and Paying Your Taxes

You can save time, money, and aggravation by being careful about how and when you file and pay your taxes, and how you deal with Revenue Canada. This chapter will help you handle these matters effectively, before you file, when you file and after you file your tax return.

One of the easiest ways to save money is to observe Revenue Canada's payment and filing requirements. Interest and penalties can leave you with a significant and avoidable bill. Daily compounding can quickly double your tax liability. There is little point in conscientious tax planning if you fail to file or pay your taxes on time.

Tax Tip

The interest provisions are a two-way street: refunds due to you from Revenue Canada as a result of overpayments of tax will earn interest, although to a much lesser degree than they used to. You begin to accrue interest on an overpayment only 45 days after the later of April 30 or the date you actually filed your return. While filing your return as early as possible won't necessarily earn you any interest from Revenue Canada, you should get your refund cheque sooner. Accordingly, the funds will be available sooner for you to invest or to use for other purposes.

Improving your cash flow

Interest-free loans to the government?

When you filed your income tax return in March or April, were you thrilled to find that you were getting a large refund from Revenue Canada? A tax refund is a mixed blessing; while expecting and getting a cheque in the mail is pleasant, a large tax refund normally indicates that your cash management could be better. In effect, you are making an interest-free loan to the government, because:

- you are making excessive instalment payments; or

• your employer is withholding too much tax.

Instead of having your money to use and invest throughout the year, you have been giving it to Revenue Canada for its use for what could amount to an entire year or more. When you overpay your tax, you don't get your own money back until after you have filed your tax return for a particular year and it is processed. Nor will you earn a year's interest on the money that you've "advanced". As mentioned above, Revenue Canada has an "interest free processing period" that runs 45 days from the later of April 30 and the date the return is filed. That means that if you file your return on time – on April 30 – no interest will be paid on refunds until after June 14.

Steps to take

To a large extent, you can avoid the problem and improve your cash flow.

If you pay your tax by instalments, you should be reviewing your instalment requirements throughout the year. If you made a large, perhaps unexpected, contribution to your RRSP midyear, recalculate your tax liability. It may be significantly lower than the estimate you made in March because of the RRSP contribution. Your instalments for the remainder of the year should be reduced accordingly.

If you are employed, most of your tax liability is likely satisfied through withholdings at source. If you also:

• incur business or investment losses;

• have significant deductible interest expense;

• make RRSP contributions;

• pay deductible alimony or maintenance to a former spouse; or

• have some other deductible expenditures,

consider writing to the Chief of Source Deductions at your local District Taxation Office for a waiver from or reduction in withholdings. If your request is approved, your employer will receive a letter from Revenue Canada authorizing a reduction in the amount of tax withheld from your income. This could increase your cash flow and allow you to use or invest the funds that otherwise would not be available until you get your tax refund.

Before you file

Social Insurance Number

If you lived or worked in Canada during the year and you file an income tax return, you must include your Social Insurance Number (SIN) on your return. You should also indicate your spouse's SIN on your return.

In the past, use of your SIN on information slips such as T3s, T5s, etc. was not mandatory. Now, however, if you are requested to provide your SIN to a person preparing information returns and fail to do so, you may be liable for a fine of $100 each time you do not provide it. If you do not have a SIN, you have 15 days to apply for one from the time you are requested to provide it, and a further 15 days to supply the number.

Instalment requirements

If you are earning employment income and have no other major sources of income, the amount of tax withheld at source by your employer will generally leave you with either a small refund or a small balance owing on April 30. If you have other sources of income, however, you may have to make instalments of tax during the year.

Instalments for a particular year are due on:

- March 15;

- June 15;

- September 15; and

- December 15,

with any final balance due when you file your return. Late or deficient instalments could result in onerous interest and penalty charges (see Interest and penalties, page 194).

Changes have been made to the basis for determining who is required to make quarterly income tax instalments. Quite simply, you are required to make quarterly payments if the difference between your tax payable and amounts that have been withheld at source is greater than $2,000 in both the current and either of the two preceding years.

Tax payable includes combined federal and provincial income tax. For Québec residents, the threshold amount is $1,200 of federal tax payable after federal tax withholdings.

This new system comes into effect with the September 15, 1994 instalment. As a transitional measure, the September and December 1994 instalments are to cover a maximum of one-half of the year's total instalment liability.

Revenue Canada will continue to notify individuals required to remit instalments of the amount of each instalment determined on the basis of tax information from prior years.

Individuals who are required to pay quarterly instalments should have received two notices from Revenue Canada in 1994, one in February with the March and June instalments and one in August with the September and December instalments. Here is how Revenue Canada determines the amounts:

- the first two instalments are based on your tax liability from two years ago, i.e., for 1994, each of your first two instalments would be based on one-quarter of your 1992 tax liability;

192

- the third and fourth payments are based on your liability for the preceding year, i.e., 1993 for 1994 instalments, with an adjustment to ensure that the total of the four instalments equals your prior year's liability.

If you choose to follow this new method and pay the exact amounts specified by Revenue Canada **on time**, you will not be charged interest and penalties even if your instalments are short.

Of course, the two other existing options are also available to you if you prefer to continue with the method you have used in the past:

- divide your prior year's tax liability by four and pay that amount each quarter; or

- if you are confident that your current year's liability will be less than that of the previous year, estimate the liability and pay 25% of that amount each quarter. In this case, review your situation before each payment to make sure that your original estimate is still valid.

If you choose this latter option and you estimate incorrectly, interest may be charged on the deficient instalments.

Tax Tip

Interest charges on late or deficient instalments can be significant. You can cure a deficient or late instalment payment by early payment or overpayment of the next instalment. Since interest is levied only to the extent that debit interest exceeds any credit offset, you should be able to reduce or eliminate interest charges on late or deficient instalments.

When you file

Filing on the most favourable basis

Tax laws and regulations are not always unambiguous. When filing your return you should choose the most favourable, reasonable interpretation. For example, file your current year's return reflecting the results of a favourable court decision. If your position is challenged, possibly because the case you followed is under appeal, you may have to protect the position you have taken by filing a Notice of Objection. This should enable you to sustain the claim if Revenue Canada eventually agrees with the court's decision. If the decision is subsequently overturned, at least you are in the same position you would have been in had you not made the claim. You should only be out-of-pocket to the extent of some interest charges.

Filing returns

Your income tax return each taxation year must be filed by April 30 of the following year. Unless a demand is made for your return, the penalty for late filing is based on the amount of tax payable. If you owe tax but cannot pay it on the due date, the late filing penalty will be avoided if you file your return on time. Conversely, you should face no late filing penalty if your tax is paid in full by April 30, even though you do not file the return until later.

Income from an unincorporated business or a partnership is reported in your personal return. The partnership will have to file information with Revenue Canada and provide you with a reporting slip to enclose with your return. If the business or partnership has a non-calendar year end, income from it must be included in your return for the calendar year in which the fiscal year of the business or partnership ends.

Paying your taxes

If you have a balance of tax owing for a particular year, it is due on April 30 of the following year, the same day on which your return must be filed. If you do not pay the balance by April 30, interest will be charged on the outstanding amount (see Interest and penalties, below).

If you are unable to pay taxes owing by April 30, you should include a letter with your return explaining the situation, or contact the Collections Section of your district office. Revenue Canada will generally accommodate a reasonable payment schedule. You may also include postdated cheques with your return. Again, reason should prevail: do not date your cheques two years from the time the payment is due.

After you file

Interest and penalties

Higher interest charges encourage prompt payment of taxes and instalments. The prescribed rate of interest is set every three months, based on short-term interest rates charged during a calendar quarter plus two percentage points. The higher rate applies to overdue income taxes, insufficient instalment payments, unpaid employee source deductions and other amounts withheld at source, unpaid Canada Pension Plan contributions, and unpaid unemployment insurance premiums. (The same rate of interest is also paid on refunds.)

If you file your return late, even if it is only by one day, you will be subject to a late filing penalty equal to 5% of any unpaid tax, plus 1% for each month (to a maximum of 12 months) for which you fail to file the return after the deadline. If you fail to file on time again within a three-year period, the penalty doubles to 10% plus 2% per month of the unpaid amount to a maximum of 20 months.

If you are neglecting to make instalment payments as required, and the amounts are large enough, additional penalties apply to interest in excess of $1,000 owing on late instalments.

You may be fined $100 for each instance you fail to complete all the information required of you on your return. Even a dishonoured cheque will be expensive: Revenue Canada will add $10 to your tax bill for any NSF cheque. Of course, this is in addition to the fee your bank will charge you. In extreme situations, you could be subject to fines of $1,000 to $25,000, or up to 12 months' imprisonment, or both, if you are convicted of an offence under the *Income Tax Act*.

Failure to pay your taxes on time can become a rather expensive form of financing. Interest, which is also charged on penalties assessed against you but unpaid, is compounded daily. In addition, interest and penalties are not deductible for tax purposes.

Amending returns

What if you have mailed your return and then discovered an error on the return or received additional information that will change your tax liability? You should inform Revenue Canada of the changes, but do not file a corrected return; a letter explaining the situation is all that is required. If you have received a Notice of Assessment, contact your district taxation office; otherwise, contact your regional taxation centre. Always include your SIN when corresponding with Revenue Canada, to help them find your file.

Revenue Canada will generally permit you to amend your return for errors or omissions up to three years after the date of mailing shown on the Notice of Assessment, the same time limit that the government has for reassessing your return. You should note that Revenue Canada will not entertain amending a return because you had a change of heart regarding an optional deduction.

Resolving problems

You will usually receive a Notice of Assessment from Revenue Canada within about eight to 12 weeks of filing your return. Your return may well be assessed exactly as you filed it. Often, however, you will find changes to your return. If you agree with the changes, correction of a calculation error, for example, you should pay any additional tax owing as soon as possible to avoid interest charges.

If you disagree with the way in which your return has been assessed, remember that you are technically bound by the Notice of Assessment unless you object to it. Should you disagree with the Notice of Assessment, you might pursue one of two courses. The simplest course is to contact your district taxation office, by phone or in person. Have your Social Insurance Number handy. In many instances, problems can be readily explained or resolved on the spot.

You may have to follow a more elaborate procedure if:

• you have postponed getting in touch with Revenue Canada;

• significant amounts of money are involved; or

• you feel the matter is quite complex.

In any of these cases, you should consider filing a Notice of Objection to your assessment. A Notice of Objection may be filed on a prescribed form (Form T400A, which you may obtain from your district taxation office). Alternatively, you may initiate the appeal process by setting out the facts and reasons for your objection in a letter to the Chief of Appeals at your local district office or taxation centre. The limit for objection for individuals and testamentary trusts is the later of one year after the balance due day for your return for the year (for example, May 1, 1996 for your 1994 return, which is due April 30, 1995) and 90 days after the mailing date indicated on your assessment.

Revenue Canada is generally under no obligation to entertain any objections you may have to your assessment if you miss the deadline.

Your return will be reviewed and if Revenue Canada agrees with your position, you will receive a revised Notice of Reassessment. If Revenue Canada disagrees, you will receive notification that the assessment stands. While you may prepare a Notice of Objection yourself, you should consider seeking professional advice, particularly if the amount of tax at stake is significant.

If you still disagree, or if you have not heard from Revenue Canada within 90 days of filing your objection, you may appeal to the courts. However, before proceeding beyond the objection stage, you should talk to your professional advisor. Interest on any unpaid tax continues to accrue during the time your appeal is in process unless you post acceptable security while your objection is still in process. You may also pay the amount in dispute and wait for a possible refund if the matter is resolved in your favour.

If you appeal to the Tax Court of Canada and the amount in dispute is less than $12,000, an informal appeal procedure is available. You may represent yourself or have your lawyer or accountant or other agent represent you. The appeal process should take about six months. If the amount in dispute exceeds $12,000, general court rules apply. You can still represent yourself, but this is not advisable unless you are well versed in both the *Income Tax Act* and legal procedure.

Further appeals can be made to higher courts: the Federal Court of Appeal and even to the Supreme Court of Canada. The Supreme Court, however, may refuse to grant leave to hear your appeal. Your legal advisor will help you determine whether you have a case, what your chances of success are, and how expensive the whole procedure is likely to be.

Tax Tip

Even if your problem has been satisfactorily resolved by phone or in a personal visit to your District Taxation Office, you should note the deadline for filing a Notice of Objection. If you have not received a revised assessment or a Notice of Reassessment by a week or two before the deadline for filing an objection, consider filing a Notice of Objection in any event to protect your position, particularly if substantial amounts are involved.

Post-assessment examination

The Notice of Assessment that Revenue Canada issues is based on a limited review of your return when it is filed. Once the assessment has been issued, your return may be subject to further examination. Two main types of reviews can be carried out after your return has been assessed:

- Information slips received by Revenue Canada from your employer, from banks, and other financial institutions, from the trustee of your RRSP, etc., are matched with your Social Insurance Number to ensure that you have reported all of your employment and investment income.

- The various expenses, deductions, and credits that you claimed may be subject to further review. You may be asked to provide receipts and other documentation to support your claims. Be sure to keep your supporting documents in case your return is selected for review.

Although any return can be selected for detailed examination, the probability increases with the magnitude of the amounts and the nature of income and expense items. In any case, recognize that if you report income from business or property, your return may be selected for a full audit. If you are going to be audited, you will generally be asked to gather all the information that you used to prepare your return and to meet with a Revenue Canada representative. You may bring your professional advisor with you; it is recommended that you do so if your return was prepared by your advisor. The auditor will go through your return with you, examine your supporting documentation and ask questions. As long as you are able to substantiate all of the items on your return, you should not have any problems.

If the auditor proposes any changes to your return and you disagree, you will have to go through the appeal process, beginning with the filing of a Notice of Objection, as described above.

Fairness Package for taxpayers

The Fairness Package is legislation designed to improve the fairness of the tax system for all Canadians. The Fairness Package contains measures aimed at taxpayers who, because of personal misfortune or circumstances beyond their control, are unable to meet filing or payment deadlines or comply with certain rules. Interest or penalties may be waived or cancelled when they result from factors that are beyond your control, for example, where an illness prevents you from filing a tax return by the April 30 deadline. Of course, you are expected to have made reasonable efforts to comply with the law, to minimize delays in filing a return, and to remedy the situation as soon as possible.

In the past, if you wanted to claim a refund in respect of a particular taxation year, you had to do so within three years of that year. Now, in certain circumstances, individuals and testamentary trusts may file for refunds for any taxation year after 1984 without regard to the three-year limitation. Refunds may be allowed where an individual or a testamentary trust files a return for the first time or requests a reassessment. In particular, you may be able to obtain a refund or a reduction in taxes owing if:

- your taxes have been overpaid because of the amount of tax withheld at source by your employer;

- you have neglected to claim refundable tax credits; or

- you previously filed your return and then discovered that a deduction to which you were entitled had been missed.

You may not, however, request an increase in deductions such as capital cost allowance, to generate a refund.

The *Income Tax Act* contains more than 120 elections that let taxpayers select from specified options how the tax laws will apply to their financial affairs for income tax purposes. The fairness legislation gives the Minister discretionary power to allow you to apply to make a late or amended "election" or to revoke an original election for taxation years back to 1985. This discretion is not intended to permit retroactive tax planning. The elections initially eligible for this treatment are set out in an Income Tax Regulation; others will be added as they are identified.

Books and records

You should keep your tax records for at least four years (approximately the period during which Revenue Canada can reassess your return), and preferably longer. If you operate a business, you must keep your tax and business records for at least six years, and even then you may still have to seek permission from Revenue Canada to destroy them.

Directors' tax risks

You should not accept an appointment as a director of a corporation lightly. In addition to the obligations and responsibilities that you take on as a director, you may find that you are financially at risk. As a director, you face two kinds of tax risks. First, you may be liable for income tax on your director's fees even though the corporation withholds tax from the payments you receive. If the corporation cannot satisfy the tax liability in respect of your income, you may be liable. In effect you will be taxed twice. If you have any doubt about the financial security of the corporation, be sure to satisfy yourself that the corporation is handling the withheld taxes properly.

Potentially more onerous than double taxation on your director's fees is your possible liability for corporate income taxes, Canada Pension Plan payments, and Unemployment Insurance contributions.

Directors of corporations may be jointly and severally liable, together with their corporation, for amounts the corporation has failed to withhold and remit to the Receiver General, as well as for any related interest and penalties. Directors' liability also extends to amounts required to be withheld and remitted under the Canada Pension Plan and the *Unemployment Insurance Act*.

Over the past few years, Revenue Canada has actively prosecuted corporate directors for failure of the corporation to remit payroll deductions. The cases do not reveal any clear-cut threshold of activity a director must undertake to meet the requirements of due diligence. Revenue Canada has basically taken the position that directors may be absolved of personal liability if they are found to have exercised the degree of care, diligence and skill to prevent the failure that a reasonably prudent person would have exercised in comparable circumstances. To protect yourself, you must ensure that the system of withholding and remitting source deductions is well-established and functioning properly. And bear in mind that ignorance of the law does not appear to be a defence.

Tax Tip

No action can be initiated against a former director more than two years after he or she ceases to be a director. Accordingly, if you are currently a director, consider resigning if the corporation of which you are a director is in serious trouble. As an added precaution, also consider registering your resignation with the appropriate corporate registry.

⚜ **Québec**

If you have to deal with Revenue Québec, you should be aware of the following:

Before you file

In Québec, beginning with the September 1994 instalment, tax instalments will be required when the difference between Québec tax payable (net of the reduction) and Québec tax deducted at source exceeds $1,200 for the current year and either of the two preceding years.

After you file

Interest on refunds starts the 46th day after the later of:

• April 30; and

• the date you file your return.

Furthermore, as set out in the table on page 63, the interest rate paid on refunds is significantly lower (4.5% lower for the fourth quarter of 1994) than the interest rate charged on amounts due.

• Interest and penalties

The penalty charge by Revenue Québec for NSF cheques is $35. Revenue Québec has introduced a penalty for late filing of a return equal to 5% of unpaid taxes. An additional penalty of 1% is added for each month of late filing (up to a maximum of 12 months).

If you have neglected to make your Québec instalment payments, an additional interest of 10% per year is applied only if instalments are less than 90% of the required instalments. This interest is added to the normal interest rate on receivables that Revenue Québec charges.

Other increases have been planned to enable the Ministère du Revenu du Québec to collect more money.

• Resolving problems

Québec follows the same rules as other jurisdictions for resolving problems, except that in Québec:

- The Ministère du Revenu has confirmed that is now possible to file a Notice of Objection by mailing a single copy of a letter to the person in charge of such notices (the "directeur des oppositions").

- If you receive notification that the assessment stands after you have filed your Notice of Objection or if you have not heard from Revenue Québec within 90 days of filing your Notice of Objection, you may appeal to the courts.

- You can appeal successively to:

  - the Québec Court (civil division);

  - the Québec Court of Appeal; and

  - the Supreme Court of Canada.

An individual can also bring his or her case before the Small Claims Court. Doing so waives the right to any remedy before any other court.

An individual can also go to the complaints office of Revenue Québec. The brochure entitled A New Mechanism for Resolving Tax Problems: The Bureau des Plaintes of Revenu Québec (INF-138) explains how an individual can submit a complaint in writing to this new service of Revenue Québec.

Québec has not agreed to fully harmonize the equity measures introduced at the federal level. Thus, although currently Revenue Québec can reopen statute-barred years according to law, it has refused to do so in many instances.

Looking Ahead

Looking Ahead

Your personal tax strategy should include looking into the future. You need to consider your own tax affairs and concerns, as well as anticipated changes in the tax system. This chapter briefly reviews both aspects of looking ahead.

Your own tax affairs

Tax planning is not something that you start to think about in December. With the exception of your RRSP contribution, which you can make within the first 60 days of the next year, all is pretty much said and done by December 31. The earlier in the year that you start your tax planning, the more opportunities you will have to act on some of the ideas in this book and to minimize your tax liability. While you may not need a great deal of time to put some of these suggestions into place, others will require lead time. Keeping your records organized should allow you to identify opportunities and to minimize the risk of making costly mistakes such as underpaying your instalments.

The rest of 1994 and into 1995

• Eliminating CNIL problems

If you are planning to take advantage of the enhanced lifetime capital gains exemption this year (page 93), or will be making a special election on your 1994 tax return (page 93), ensure that your ability to access the exemption is not reduced or delayed because you have a CNIL. You still have time to restructure borrowings or the ownership of some investments and eliminate your CNILs (see page 122).

Tax Tip
If you have CNILs and also are the controlling shareholder of a corporation, consider paying yourself a sufficient dividend to cure your CNIL problem.

• Reviewing your instalment payments

Review your tax position prior to making the third and final instalments for the year to ensure that you are not offside. If you find that your tax liability will be larger than expected, you should consider increasing your payments, unless you have chosen to make your instalments based on Revenue Canada's instalment requirements (see page 190).

• Spousal RRSPs

Making a contribution to a spousal RRSP based on your own contribution entitlement is still one of the most effective ways of income splitting. In addition, if you are receiving periodic pension income from an RPP or DPSP, you can transfer up to $6,000 per annum to a spousal RRSP. 1994 is the last year in which you will be able to take advantage of this special rule.

• Salary/dividend mix

If you are a controlling shareholder of a private company, you are likely in a position to decide what type of compensation you will receive. In choosing between salary and dividends, you should ensure that you are receiving at least enough salary to permit you to make maximum contributions to your RRSP (see page 26).

Tax Tip

Your RRSP contribution limit in 1995 will be based on 1994 earned income. To make the maximum contribution next year, you will need $80,556 of earned income in 1994.

• Pension income credit

If you are age 65 or over and are not taking advantage of the pension income credit, consider arranging to receive eligible pension income, perhaps by converting a portion of your RRSP to a retirement income stream that will provide you with at least $1,000 of eligible pension income (see page 134).

208 • **Lifetime capital gains exemption**

Draft legislation that enacts the 1994 federal budget proposals will eliminate the $100,000 lifetime capital gains exemption for gains realized or accrued after February 22, 1994. If you still have capital gains exemption available, however, you may be able to take advantage of a special election that will allow you to use some or all of that unused exemption. You must make the election on your 1994 income tax return (due on April 30, 1995) or else the exemption will be lost to you forever (see page 93 for details).

• **"Junior" tax returns**

When you are in the midst of preparing to file your income tax returns, consider encouraging your children who are over age 18 (or younger if they have sufficient income) to file their own income tax returns. University students often fail to file tax returns, since the credit for tuition fees offsets tax that would be payable on any income earned (or the tuition fee credit may have been transferred to you as a supporting person). The child is foregoing credits to which he or she may be entitled by not filing a return. Further, the financial benefits are not the only reason that young adults should be filing their own returns. There are probably many young adults who have their own credit cards, yet know little about the procedures and consequences involved in filing an income tax return. This would be an excellent opportunity to begin to shift the burden of responsibility to these young adults for their own financial affairs.

Tax Tip

Young adults age 19 or over may claim their own GST credit (even if they have no income), as well as any provincial credits that may be available and that can be claimed only by filing an income tax return.

• Home Buyers' Plan

The Home Buyers' Plan (the "Plan") was originally introduced as a temporary measure to allow individuals to use existing funds in their RRSPs to purchase a home. The Plan was scheduled to expire on March 2, 1994. The 1994 federal budget proposed to modify the Plan so that it will continue for first-time home buyers only. The modified Plan took effect on March 2, 1994. Of course, you may not participate in the modified Plan if you or your spouse withdrew funds under the previous Plan. If you applied to participate in the Home Buyers' Plan before March 2, 1994 and you actually received the funds before April 1994, you are subject to the rules under the former Plan.

You are considered to be a first-time home buyer if neither you nor your spouse, during your marriage, owned a home and lived in it as your principal place of residence at any time in the period beginning on January 1st of the fourth calendar year before the withdrawal and ending on the 31st day before the withdrawal from your RRSP. Further, you may participate in the Home Buyers' Plan only once.

A qualifying home must be located in Canada and cannot have been previously owned by you or your spouse. You must intend to occupy it as your principal place of residence no later than one year after its acquisition. Both new and existing homes are eligible and all types of structures are included in the definition: a detached house; a semi-detached house; a townhouse; a condominium; a mobile home; an apartment in a duplex, triplex, fourplex or apartment building; and even a share in a co-operative housing corporation.

You may withdraw up to $20,000 from your RRSP (up to $40,000 per couple) free of tax. You may acquire a qualifying home either on your own or jointly with one or more other persons. A husband and wife may each withdraw $20,000 from their own RRSPs as long as they own the home jointly. If you contributed $20,000 to your own plan and $20,000 to your spouse's plan, you may each withdraw $20,000 to jointly acquire a home. If you did not contribute to your own plan, but contributed $40,000 to a spousal plan, your spouse can withdraw no more than $20,000, even if you are acquiring the property jointly.

You must repay your RRSP the funds withdrawn for this purpose in at least 15 annual equal instalments. If you withdraw funds from your RRSP under the modified Plan, i.e., after March 1, 1994, the 15-year repayment period will begin in the second calendar year following the year in which the withdrawal is made. In addition, you must purchase a qualifying home before October 1 of the calendar year following the year of withdrawal. For example, if you made a Home Buyers' Plan withdrawal of $15,000 on April 15, 1994, you have until October 1, 1995 to acquire a qualifying home and your first annual repayment of $1,000 will be due by the end of 1996. You may elect to have a repayment made in the first 60 days of a year treated as having been made in the preceding year. Of course, if you repay more than the minimum amount in a particular year, in the following year your payment would be based on the amount left to be repaid, divided by the number of years left in the 15-year repayment period. If you fail to meet the repayment schedule or fall short of a payment in a particular year, the unrepaid amount will be added to your income and, accordingly, will be subject to tax at your marginal tax rate.

To request a withdrawal from your RRSP under the Home Buyers' Plan, you must complete a prescribed form (T1036). The form details the location of the qualifying home and confirms that you intend to use that home as your principal place of residence no later than one year after its acquisition. Prior to receiving funds from your RRSP, you must have entered into an agreement in writing for the acquisition or construction of the qualifying home.

If you withdraw funds in accordance with the Home Buyers' Plan but the purchase doesn't go through for some reason, you won't be penalized with an income inclusion, provided that you return the funds to your RRSP by the end of the following year.

You will not be able to claim a tax deduction for contributions to your RRSP that are withdrawn within 90 days under the Home

Buyers' Plan. For purposes of this rule, contributions to your RRSP within the 90-day period will not be considered to be withdrawn except to the extent that the RRSP balance after the withdrawals is less than the amount of such contributions. Of course, your RRSP room in that period will not be lost; you will be able to carry it forward for use in future years (see page 26).

If you make an RRSP contribution and later decide to participate in the plan, you will be permitted to withdraw the contribution to purchase your home, but you won't get a tax deduction for it.

The longer term: estate planning

Two common misconceptions are associated with the term estate planning: the first is that it is something to be worried about sometime in the future when you are "older"; the second is that significant amounts of money must be involved. The fact is that while you may not have a formal estate plan in mind at the tender age of 21, everyone over the age of majority should give some thought to the consequences of their death, particularly if there are any dependants. You should, however, be wary of carrying out plans for the transfer of your wealth until your own position is secure and you are confident of the ability of your intended beneficiaries to deal with the implications.

An estate plan can be as simple or as elaborate as you wish. Your circumstances and financial situation will, of course, affect the complexity of your estate plan. The size of your estate should not be an issue either: we are all concerned with ensuring that we will be able to maintain our life-styles after retirement, that our dependants will be taken care of in the event of our death, and that our assets will be distributed on our death according to our wishes.

Estate planning is not something that you do once and for all. Rather, it should be a continuing process of evaluating your personal and business circumstances and directing the manner in which your assets are preserved and ultimately distributed.

To remain effective, your estate plan should be reviewed periodically and revised to accommodate changes in your financial and
personal life or in legislation, including taxation.

• Insurance

Choosing the appropriate insurance program may satisfy a variety of
objectives. The most important one is to provide your spouse and
children with a replacement for the income that is lost on your death
and to provide them with the funds necessary to cover the payment
of income taxes and other debts and expenses arising on death.
Some forms of life insurance policies are looked on as investments as
well as providing protection. An exempt life insurance policy provides an opportunity to accommodate investment on a favourable
tax basis. As with other investments, tax consequences should not
be the primary concern in evaluating the opportunity and rates of
return should be carefully considered. However, the low rate of tax
applicable to exempt policy earnings and the possibility of receiving
the benefit of the policy free of tax (during life as well as on death)
may make this a worthwhile option in some circumstances. Your
professional advisors can tell you what types of whole life insurance
policies are exempt.

In business situations, insurance may be used to provide funding
for the eventual purchase of assets or shares in connection with a
buy-out of partners or partners' heirs.

Insurance proceeds that are payable as a result of the death of the
insured are not taxable in the hands of the beneficiary.

• Up-to-date wills

Dying intestate (without a will) can defeat almost all the estate planning arrangements you have worked hard to put into place. Provincial laws dictate how your assets are to be divided if you do not have
a will.

Tax Tip

Both you and your spouse should have a will. This is probably one of the most critical elements of your estate planning program.

Your will should be reviewed at least every five years by your lawyer and also by your professional tax advisor if your affairs have become at all complex. Your lawyer will suggest any necessary changes. It should also be reassessed in light of changes in the law, particularly family law. In some provinces, the law virtually dictates how family assets are to be divided even if you have drafted a comprehensive will. It should certainly be reviewed if your personal or financial circumstances have changed. For example, your will is invalid if you subsequently become divorced. Your will should be reviewed if you get married, if you adopt a child, if one of your beneficiaries dies, and even if you make a large tax-free transfer to your RRSP.

• Estate freezing

In many ways, estate freezing is an extension of income splitting. The idea behind this type of planning is to transfer any future growth in the value of an asset (and any tax liability on future appreciation) to your heirs. Ideally, however, you would retain control over the asset during your lifetime. In an estate freeze, the value of an asset to you is frozen for tax purposes. In so doing, an immediate tax liability could result because you may have to recognize a capital gain when ownership of the asset is transferred. To the extent that you have not exhausted it, however, the capital gain would be eligible for the enhanced $400,000 capital gains exemption. Even if the exemption is not available, other deferral methods are.

Estate freezes are often executed using a corporation, rather than through a direct sale or transfer to an intended beneficiary. Tax can be deferred, minimized, or even eliminated. Ownership of the shares in the corporation should be structured so as to ensure that growth in the value of assets accrues to your heirs, while you retain control over the corporation, and accordingly over the assets, during your lifetime. Generally, personal assets can be transferred into a corporation with no immediate tax consequences, the corporation being considered to acquire the assets at your cost.

Estate freezing is complex. You should discuss any ideas or concerns you might have with your professional tax advisor.

• Offshore protection trusts

Offshore protection trusts are becoming increasingly popular vehicles for affluent individuals who might be exposed to personal liability in a potential lawsuit. If your situation is such that you might be at risk, you might look to transferring assets offshore to jurisdictions like the Bahamas, the Channel Islands, the Cayman Islands, or other such exotic havens, to protect your assets from the claims of creditors in Canada.

The idea is that if assets are held in a jurisdiction where a Canadian judgment is not recognized (or even where the domestic judgment is enforceable), the cost and difficulty associated with taking action in a foreign court would discourage a creditor from pursuing the matter.

Offshore trusts are also being used by individuals concerned with protecting assets in the event of divorce or death.

When you are setting up the trust, there must be no claims or potential claims in the offing. You must be solvent, and must have no intent to defraud any of your creditors at the time of setting up your protective offshore trust.

In order for an offshore protection trust arrangement to make sense, an individual should have at least half a million dollars of liquid and easily movable assets available for transfer. Of course, there are fees associated with setting up the trust, as well as annual administration costs.

A final caveat: the use of an offshore trust may help you protect your assets, but it won't help you escape Revenue Canada. Canadian residents are taxable on their worldwide income. Accordingly, any income that is earned on assets in the offshore trust will still be taxable in your hands.

• Taxes on death

There are no federal or provincial death taxes per se in Canada. Generally, however, you are deemed to have disposed of all of your capital property immediately prior to death for proceeds equal to the fair market value of the assets at that time. Any capital gains that have accrued to the date of death would be included and taxed in your final income tax return, with one major exception: unless you elect otherwise, all assets passing to your spouse or a spousal trust are transferred at cost, with the spouse or spousal trust inheriting your cost base. Accordingly, no immediate income tax consequences result. But assets passing to anyone else, including a trust, are subject to the deemed disposition rules.

Tax Tip

To the extent that it has not been exhausted, the enhanced $400,000 capital gains exemption may shelter any capital gains arising on qualified small business corporation shares or qualified farm property as a result of the deemed disposition rules. In addition, the AMT provisions are not applicable in the year of death.

The executors of your estate will be responsible for payment of any taxes owing on your final income tax return and for taxes payable on income earned on your assets before they are distributed to your beneficiaries.

Tax Tip

In addition to a final return of income, the executor of an estate may choose to file up to three additional separate returns in respect of certain types of income that have been earned but unrealized at the date of death. Full personal tax credits may be claimed for each of the separate returns, which could result in substantial tax savings.

Changes to the tax system

Changes to the tax system result from changes in federal and provincial legislation and regulations, new interpretations resulting from court decisions, and administrative changes by Revenue Canada. Changes to federal legislation can be made through federal budgets, as well as technical amendment bills. Technical amendment bills tend to be somewhat predictable.

Court decisions are less predictable, but important new interpretations are usually reported in the popular press. Revenue Canada can change its interpretation at any time through press releases, interpretation bulletins, and information circulars.

This book reflects changes in income tax to August 31, 1994 and includes tax laws that have been passed up to that date, as well as changes proposed in the 1994 federal budget. Provincial governments generally present their budgets in late winter or spring. Of course, governments can deviate from this pattern and may bring down budgets at any time. When *Personal Tax Strategy* was written, all the provinces and territories had brought down their 1994-95 budgets. Personal income tax changes introduced in those budgets are reflected in this book.

Income taxes for the provinces and territories (other than Québec, which collects its own tax) are currently calculated as a percentage of federal rates; the federal government collects income taxes on their behalf. Apparently, there is a possibility that the provinces and territories may be permitted to set provincial tax rates independent of federal rates and to collect those taxes themselves. This could lead to a more complex array of income taxes across Canada, although for most individuals the most visible change would likely be the requirement to file separate federal and provincial/territorial income tax returns.

Technical amendments can be extremely important for a few tax-payers, and insignificant to others, although some technical amendments have broader application. Your professional advisor can help you determine whether this year's technical amendments affect you.

Appendices

Appendix 1
Combined marginal rates

This appendix will help you:
- determine your 1994 marginal tax rate
- compare tax rates in Canada

Combined marginal rates are the total of federal marginal rates (Appendix 4) and provincial marginal rates (Appendix 5), including federal and provincial surtaxes.

The combined marginal rates shown in this appendix apply to most income. Appendix 3 shows top marginal rates for certain **investment income.**

Your marginal rate is the highest marginal rate that applies to you, because it is the percentage of any additional taxable income that you will pay as income tax. If your marginal rate is 49%, then 49% of the last dollar you earned, and of any additional income you earn, will go to pay income taxes.

Your marginal rate also measures the value of any deduction from taxable income. At a 49% marginal rate, a $100 deduction reduces your tax bill by $49.

Taxable income is your income from all sources, less deductions (see page 164).

The chart shows a range of taxable income, starting at zero on the left, and ending at an amount over $100,000. (Above that level no additional tax brackets exist, so you can imagine the bars continuing indefinitely to the right.) Taxable income is drawn to scale.

The jurisdictions are in descending order: British Columbia has the highest top marginal rate, (54.16%) for 1994, so it appears first. The Northwest Territories, with the lowest top marginal rate (44.37%), appears last. This arrangement, with taxable income drawn to scale and provinces listed in order of decreasing top marginal rate, is used in most of the appendices to Personal Tax Strategy.)

To find your marginal tax rate, simply look for the jurisdiction in which you reside. (Rates for nonresidents are also given.) Then move across the chart to the box that corresponds to your taxable income.

The rates shown here **include the provincial tax reductions** that Alberta, British Columbia, Manitoba, Ontario, Saskatchewan and – starting in 1994 – Québec have. Except for Québec, the reductions normally affect

A1

1994 Combined marginal rates [including all surtaxes]

Taxable income → — $0, $6,456, $29,590, $59,180, $62,195 ... $100,000

Highest Top Marginal Rate → Lowest Top Marginal Rate

Provincial tax as % of basic federal tax	Province	Combined marginal rates (low income → high income)
52.5%	British Columbia*	17.51%*, 26.44%, 28.44%*, 26.44%, 40.43%, 44.53%, 49.66%, 51.11%, 54.16%
59.5%	Nova Scotia	0%, 27.63%, 42.25%, 47.13%, 50.58%, 52.03%, 53.75%
58%	Ontario*	17.51%*, 27.37%, 47.09%*, 41.86%, 44.88%, 51.50%, 50.05%, 53.19%
n/a	Québec*	14.71%, 34.09%*, 36.13%*, 38.17%*, 47.12%*, 45.95%*, 48.19%*, 48.89%, 51.49%, 52.94%
50%	Saskatchewan*	17.51%*, 34.06%*, 29.06%, 29.06%, 43.28%, 45.53%, 50.50%, 51.95%
64%	New Brunswick	28.39%, 43.42%, 48.43%, 49.88%, 51.36%
69%	Newfoundland	0%, 29.24%, 44.72%, 49.88%, 51.33%
52%	Manitoba*	17.51%*, 30.35%*, 28.35%, 42.30%, 44.30%, 48.95%, 50.40%
59.5%	Prince Edward Island	27.63%, 42.25%, 47.13%, 48.58%, 50.30%
50%	Yukon	26.01%, 39.78%, 44.37%, 45.10%, 46.55%
52%	Non-resident	0%, 26.35%, 40.30%, 44.95%, 46.40%
45.5%	Alberta*	17.51%*, 29.86%*, 25.75%, 39.11%, 40.06%, 44.62%, 46.07%
45%	Northwest Territories**	24.54%**, 24.66%**, 37.98%**, 38.11%**, 42.55%***, 44.00%***, 44.37%

Taxable income → — $0, $10,000, $20,000, $30,000, $40,000, $50,000, $60,000, $70,000, $80,000, $90,000, $100,000

* Provincial tax reductions in Alberta, British Columbia, Manitoba, Ontario, and Saskatchewan will alter the marginal rates for low-income taxpayers. Québec taxpayers with incomes up to about $53,000 are affected. Brackets affected by or created by tax reductions are marked by grey lines.

** The results reflect the Northwest Territories' Cost of Living Tax Credit, which reduces tax payable and creates additional brackets.

Appendix 1
Combined marginal rates

only taxpayers in the lowest income brackets. Reductions are discussed in Appendix 5.

Top marginal rates are in bold type toward the right of the table. Top marginal rates are also shown in the bar chart in Appendix 3.

To see how your marginal rate derives from federal and provincial taxes and surtaxes, refer to Appendices 4 and 5. As explained in Appendix 5, except for Québec, provincial income taxes are simply a proportion of basic federal tax. Each jurisdiction sets its own proportion. This proportion (or factor) is shown at the left of the table.

Appendix 2
How much tax?

This appendix will help you:
• estimate your 1994 income tax
• compare taxes across Canada

The big question is always: How much tax?

The table shows the total income tax payable by a person whose only tax credit is the basic nonrefundable personal credit and who has no income from Canadian dividends. Amounts shown **include all surtaxes, provincial tax reductions, and the Northwest Territories' cost of Living Tax Credit** (see Appendices 1, 4, and 5).

An **effective rate of tax** (total tax as a percentage of taxable income) is also given in the table.

The column at the extreme right repeats the **top marginal rates** that appear in Appendices 1 and 3. As taxable income gets larger, the effective rate approaches the marginal rate, so this column also represents the effective rate for an infinite (!) taxable income.

The table should be read with care. If you have tax credits other than the basic personal credit, or if your income includes Canadian dividends, your tax will be lower than the amount shown.

You can **estimate your income tax liability** in several ways. For example:

• multiply your taxable income by an effective rate interpolated from those in the table; or

• interpolate the amount of tax from those in the table.

1994 Income tax payable and effective rates

	$10,000	$25,000	$50,000	$100,000	$150,000	$200,000	$250,000	$300,000	$500,000	$1,000,000	Top rate	
					Taxable Income							
British Columbia	$890.00 / 8.87%	$4,900 / 19.61%	$14,400 / 28.73%	$39,800 / 39.80%	$66,900 / 44.59%	$94,000 / 46.98%	$121,000 / 48.42%	$148,100 / 49.37%	$256,400 / 51.29%	$527,200 / 52.72%	54.16%	Highest Top Marginal Rate
Nova Scotia	$980.00 / 9.79%	$5,120 / 20.49%	$15,000 / 30.03%	$40,400 / 40.42%	$67,300 / 44.86%	$94,200 / 47.08%	$121,000 / 48.42%	$147,900 / 49.31%	$255,400 / 51.08%	$524,200 / 52.42%	53.75%	
Ontario	$970.00 / 9.70%	$5,080 / 20.30%	$14,900 / 29.75%	$40,500 / 40.51%	$67,100 / 44.73%	$93,700 / 46.85%	$120,300 / 48.11%	$146,900 / 48.96%	$253,300 / 50.65%	$519,200 / 51.92%	53.19%	
Québec	$840.00 / 8.41%	$6,220 / 24.88%	$17,560 / 35.13%	$43,600 / 43.60%	$70,100 / 46.71%	$96,500 / 48.27%	$123,000 / 49.20%	$149,500 / 49.82%	$255,300 / 51.07%	$520,000 / 52.00%	52.94%	
Saskatchewan	$960.00 / 9.62%	$5,520 / 22.09%	$15,900 / 31.86%	$41,300 / 41.27%	$67,200 / 44.83%	$93,200 / 46.61%	$119,200 / 47.68%	$145,200 / 48.39%	$249,100 / 49.81%	$508,800 / 50.88%	51.95%	
New Brunswick	$1,010.00 / 10.06%	$5,260 / 21.06%	$15,400 / 30.86%	$39,900 / 39.85%	$65,500 / 43.69%	$91,200 / 45.61%	$116,900 / 46.76%	$142,600 / 47.53%	$245,300 / 49.06%	$502,100 / 50.21%	51.36%	
Newfoundland	$1,040.00 / 10.36%	$5,420 / 21.69%	$15,900 / 31.78%	$40,900 / 40.91%	$66,600 / 44.38%	$92,200 / 46.12%	$117,900 / 47.16%	$143,600 / 47.86%	$246,200 / 49.25%	$502,900 / 50.29%	51.33%	
Manitoba	$900.00 / 9.04%	$5,390 / 21.55%	$15,700 / 31.44%	$40,500 / 40.32%	$65,500 / 43.68%	$90,700 / 45.36%	$115,900 / 46.37%	$141,100 / 47.04%	$241,900 / 48.38%	$493,900 / 49.39%	50.40%	
Prince Edward Island	$980.00 / 9.79%	$5,120 / 20.49%	$15,000 / 30.03%	$38,800 / 38.82%	$64,000 / 42.65%	$89,100 / 44.56%	$114,300 / 45.71%	$139,400 / 46.47%	$240,000 / 48.01%	$491,500 / 49.15%	50.30%	
Yukon	$920.00 / 9.22%	$4,820 / 19.29%	$14,100 / 28.27%	$36,700 / 36.73%	$60,000 / 40.00%	$83,300 / 41.64%	$106,600 / 42.62%	$129,800 / 43.27%	$222,900 / 44.58%	$455,600 / 45.56%	46.55%	
Non-resident	$930.00 / 9.34%	$4,890 / 19.55%	$14,300 / 28.64%	$36,900 / 36.92%	$60,100 / 40.08%	$83,300 / 41.66%	$106,500 / 42.61%	$129,700 / 43.24%	$222,500 / 44.50%	$454,500 / 45.45%	46.40%	
Alberta	$680.00 / 6.77%	$4,810 / 19.23%	$14,000 / 28.05%	$36,500 / 36.47%	$59,500 / 39.67%	$82,500 / 41.27%	$105,600 / 42.23%	$128,600 / 42.87%	$220,700 / 44.15%	$451,100 / 45.11%	46.07%	
Northwest Territories	$830.00 / 8.29%	$4,530 / 18.10%	$13,400 / 26.82%	$35,000 / 34.95%	$57,100 / 38.09%	$79,300 / 39.66%	$101,500 / 40.60%	$123,700 / 41.23%	$212,400 / 42.49%	$434,300 / 43.43%	44.37%	Lowest Top Marginal Rate

Tax is rounded to the nearest $10 in the first two columns, and to the $100 in the others. Effective rates are rounded to the nearest hundredth of a percent.

Because Québec has a different system of calculating provincial tax, comparisons must be made with care. Allowable deductions n Québec will generally yield a lower taxable income than residents elsewhere in Canada would have, given the same total income.

Appendix 3
Investment income: special rates

Some investment income is taxed differently from other income. The bar chart in this appendix shows **top marginal rates** for the three types of investment income.

Interest and foreign dividends are taxed the same way as most other income. For more details about the rates that apply to interest and foreign dividends, refer to Appendix 1.

Canadian dividends are subject to a gross-up and a tax credit, which together reduce tax (see page 82).

Capital gains also get favourable tax treatment: only three-quarters of a capital gain is included in taxable income and taxed. That portion is taxed at the same rate as interest, so for most purposes the effect is tax at three-quarters the rate that applies to interest. The lifetime exemption, which was discontinued as of February 22, 1994 (see page 93), may eliminate tax on $100,000 of capital gains. Qualifying small business corporation (QSBC) shares and certain farming properties may be entitled to an exemption of $500,000 (see page 98).

The results in this Appendix apply to **capital gains in excess of the lifetime exemption**. Capital gains that are partially or completely exempt are treated even more favourably.

The bar chart shows the variation in top marginal rates for different types of investment. In all jurisdictions, the top marginal rate for capital gains is, in effect, three-quarters of the rate for interest income. For most jurisdictions, the top marginal rate for Canadian dividends works out to approximately 67.5% of the rate for interest income. However, as the bar chart reveals, the advantage of Canadian dividends over capital gains is noticeably smaller in Québec and Saskatchewan. Québec's dividend tax credit is less generous than the provincial portion in other provinces. Saskatchewan has a large flat tax that has a side-effect of reducing the differential between Canadian dividends and capital gains. Manitoba's flat tax has a smaller effect, and Alberta's still smaller flat tax reduces the advantage of Canadian dividends only slightly.

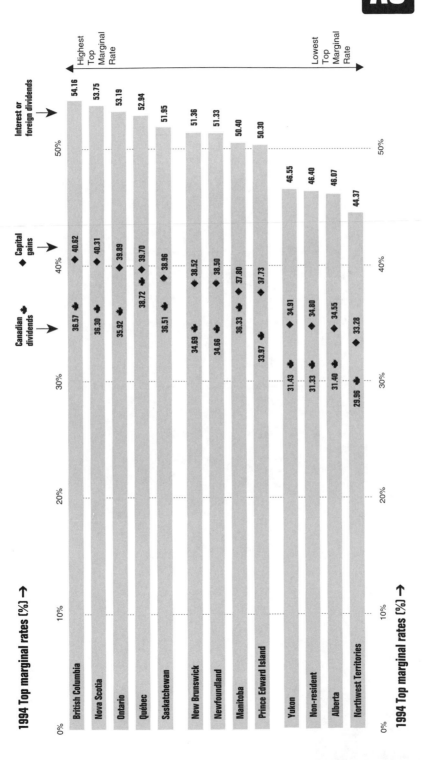

Appendix 3
Investment income: special rates

Before-tax returns required to match 6% or $100 interest

1994

	Taxable income = $50,000				Taxable income = $100,000			
	Canadian dividends		Capital gains		Canadian dividends		Capital gains	
British Columbia	4.74%	$79.03	5.13%	$85.49	4.34%	$72.27	4.63%	$77.20
Nova Scotia	4.67%	$77.76	5.07%	$84.54	4.36%	$72.60	4.65%	$77.49
Ontario	4.68%	$78.03	5.08%	$84.75	4.38%	$73.05	4.67%	$77.88
Québec	4.71%	$78.44	4.87%	$81.13	4.61%	$76.81	4.68%	$78.05
Saskatchewan	4.62%	$77.08	4.96%	$82.72	4.54%	$75.69	4.72%	$78.73
New Brunswick	4.62%	$76.92	5.03%	$83.90	4.47%	$74.46	4.75%	$79.11
Newfoundland	4.56%	$75.97	4.99%	$83.18	4.47%	$74.49	4.75%	$79.13
Manitoba	4.74%	$79.05	5.00%	$83.41	4.67%	$77.91	4.78%	$79.74
Prince Edward Island	4.67%	$77.76	5.07%	$84.54	4.52%	$75.26	4.79%	$79.81
Yukon	4.77%	$79.47	5.15%	$85.83	4.68%	$77.96	4.93%	$82.12
Non-resident	4.75%	$79.12	5.13%	$85.56	4.68%	$78.06	4.93%	$82.21
Alberta	4.78%	$79.62	5.14%	$85.69	4.72%	$78.61	4.94%	$82.40
Northwest Territories	4.85%	$80.84	5.20%	$86.66	4.77%	$79.43	5.00%	$83.38

Highest Top Marginal Rate ↑ … ↓ Lowest Top Marginal Rate

The table on page 227 shows how the different tax treatments of investments can affect investment decisions. For different types of investment, the table answers a realistic question: **What before-tax return must I get to end up with the same *after-tax* result?** As a benchmark investment, the chart assumes a 6% before-tax return in the form of interest. A $100 interest amount is included as an alternative benchmark.

For example, suppose your taxable income is in the top bracket (say $100,000) and you earn **$100 interest** on a $1,666.67 investment (a 6% before-tax return). In Ontario you would pay tax at a 53.19% marginal rate. You keep $46.81, an after-tax return of about 2.81%. To earn the identical after-tax return from the same $1,666.67 capital, you would need a **Canadian dividend of only $73.05** (which works out to 4.38%). If, instead, you had a capital gain of $77.88 on an asset you had bought for $1,666.67 a year earlier, (a 4.67% before-tax gain), you would also have a 2.81% return after tax. You would

again retain the $46.81 after tax – the same as from the $100 of interest or the $73.71 Canadian dividend.

These results vary somewhat by province, as the table shows, as well as by the taxpayer's tax bracket.

Appendix 4
Federal marginal rates: tax and surtax

This appendix will help you:
- find the federal 1994 marginal tax rate that applies to you
- see how the federal surtax affects you

Federal marginal rates are a key element in the personal income tax rate structure in Canada. Not only the federal portion of your taxes depends on federal marginal rates. Provincial and territorial income taxes are also based on federal rates (see Appendix 5). Québec is the only exception.

Your federal marginal tax rate is the percentage of the last (or next) dollar you earn that is paid as federal income tax. To find out your federal marginal rate, read the entry in the chart that corresponds to your **taxable income**.

The top portion of the chart shows the three basic federal marginal rates of 17% (on taxable income up to $29,590), 26% (on taxable income between $29,590 and $59,180) and 29% (on taxable income above $59,180). However, as the chart shows, these three rates turn into a set of five rates.

The **basic personal credit** ($1,098) eliminates tax on the first $6,456 of taxable income for all taxpayers,

creating the 0% marginal rate (because $1,098 is 17% of $6,456). This credit is indexed, increasing annually when inflation exceeds a threshold. Low inflation has kept the basic credit the same for 1994 as it was for 1993 and 1992. Any other non-refundable credits to which you may be entitled increase the amount of income on which the marginal tax rate is zero.

The general **federal surtax** rate is 3% of basic federal tax. That adds, for example, 0.51% to the 17% bottom marginal rate (17% x 3% = 0.51%). When your basic federal tax reaches $12,500, an additional "high-earner" surtax of 5% of basic federal tax in excess of $12,500 applies. This occurs at a taxable income of $62,195, assuming you have only the basic personal credit. So, at a taxable income above $62,195, the total federal surtax is 8%. Any other non-refundable credits you may be able to claim will increase the taxable income you can have before the higher "high-earner" federal surtax affects you. On account of the two levels of federal surtax, the

1994 Federal marginal rates (including the federal surtax)

Taxable income →

Except Québec

	$0 – $6,456	$6,456 – $29,590	$29,590 – $59,180	$59,180 – $62,195	$62,195 →
Before basic personal credit and federal surtax					
After basic personal credit	0%	17%	26%	29%	29%
Federal surtax rates		x 3%	x 3%	x 8% (3% + 5% "high-earner" surtax)	x 8% (3% + 5% "high-earner" surtax)
Federal surtax (addition to marginal rates)	0%	0.51%	0.78%	0.87%	2.32%
Total	0%	17.51%	26.78%	29.87%	31.32%

Québec

	$0 – $6,456	$6,456 – $29,590	$29,590 – $59,180	$59,180 – $62,195	$62,195 →
Federal rates after Québec abatement	0%	14.195% (17% x 0.835)	21.71% (26% x 0.835)	24.215% (29% x 0.835)	24.215% (29% x 0.835)
Federal surtax (addition to marginal rates)	0%	0.51%	0.78%	0.87%	2.32%
Total		14.705%	22.49%	25.085%	26.535%

Taxable income → $0, $10,000, $20,000, $30,000, $40,000, $50,000, $60,000, $70,000, $80,000, $90,000, $100,000

231

Appendix 4
Federal marginal rates: tax and surtax

29% marginal rate turns into two rates: 29.87% and 31.32%.

For Québec residents, the **Québec abatement** reduces basic federal tax by 16.5%. This, in effect, reduces federal marginal rates to 83.5% of their original levels. For example, the top federal rate of 29% becomes 24.215%. The federal surtax, however, is the same for Québec residents as it is for residents of other jurisdictions.

The federal marginal rates shown in this Appendix are central to the calculation of your tax bill. However, **the income tax you pay cannot be determined directly from federal marginal rates**. Your taxes will be substantially affected by:

• provincial taxes and surtaxes (discussed in Appendices 4 and 5), which add roughly half as much again to your tax bill.

• non-refundable tax credits to which you may be entitled (see page 166), which may reduce or even eliminate your income tax liability; and

• the types of income you have, since capital gains and some dividend income are taxed differently (see Appendix 3).

234

Appendix 5
Provincial marginal rates: tax and surtax

This appendix will help you:
- see how provincial income taxes are calculated
- see how the provincial surtaxes work

Provincial marginal rates (before surtaxes) are simply a proportion of pre-surtax federal marginal rates, except for Québec.

Québec sets its own rates and brackets. The Personal Tax Flowchart (page 167) explains how Québec's approach differs. Proposals are being discussed that would permit other provinces to introduce their own income tax systems as well.

For jurisdictions other than Québec, the proportion (or factor) is shown down the left of the chart on the facing page. The factors range from 45% in the Northwest Territories to 69% in Newfoundland. (Rates for the territories and non-residents are considered "provincial rates" in this book.) The body of the chart shows Québec's rates and the rates elsewhere (the factor multiplied by the federal marginal rates from Appendix 4).

Provinces other than Newfoundland impose provincial surtaxes. Non-residents and residents of Newfoundland or the Northwest Territories face no surtaxes other than

the federal ones.

The chart on page 237 looks complicated because it reflects the many variations in provincial surtax. It shows how much provincial tax and surtax add to marginal rates. It also shows how provincial surtaxes are calculated, and the taxable income levels to which they apply. The further to the left a bar begins, the lower the income at which the surtax first applies.

The same chart distinguishes "flat surtaxes" from surtaxes calculated as a percentage of provincial tax above some threshold. As a group, provincial surtaxes exhibit considerable complexity and variation.

Appendix 1 combines provincial taxes and surtaxes with the federal tax and the federal surtaxes set out in Appendix 4.

Alberta, British Columbia, Manitoba, Ontario, Saskatchewan, and Québec have **tax reductions** that, in effect, create additional marginal rates for those with low taxable incomes. The reductions eliminate provincial

1994 Provincial marginal rates (before surtax)

Provincial tax as % of basic federal tax

		$0	$6,456	$14,000	$23,000	$29,590	$50,000	$59,180
52.5%	British Columbia*			8.93%			13.65%	15.23%
59.5%	Nova Scotia			10.12%			15.47%	17.26%
58%	Ontario*	0%		9.86%			15.08%	16.82%
n/a	Québec*		19%	21%	23%			24%
50%	Saskatchewan*			8.5%		13%		14.5%
64%	New Brunswick			10.88%			16.64%	18.56%
69%	Newfoundland			11.73%			17.94%	20.01%
52%	Manitoba*	0%		8.84%			13.52%	15.08%
59.5%	Prince Edward Island			10.12%			15.47%	17.26%
50%	Yukon			8.5%			13%	14.5%
52%	Non-resident			8.84%			13.52%	15.08%
45.5%	Alberta*	0%		7.74%			11.83%	13.2%
45%	Northwest Territories**			7.65%			11.7%	13.05%

Taxable income →

$0 $10,000 $20,000 $30,000 $40,000 $50,000 $60,000 $70,000 $80,000 $90,000 $100,000

* Provincial tax reductions in Alberta, British Columbia, Manitoba, Ontario, and Saskatchewan will alter the marginal rates for low-income taxpayers. Québec taxpayers with incomes up to about $53,000 are affected.

** The results do not reflect the Northwest Territories' Cost of Living Tax Credit, which reduces tax payable and creates additional brackets.

Appendix 5
Provincial marginal rates: tax and surtax

income tax (but not federal income tax) for taxable incomes immediately above $6,456. However, taxpayers with slightly larger taxable incomes face a higher than normal marginal tax rate that, in effect, undoes the benefit of the provincial tax reduction. The result is that taxpayers can ignore the reductions if their taxable incomes are above a certain level (roughly $53,000 in Québec, and $10,000 to $22,000 for the other provinces that have the reductions).

Provincial surtaxes can affect marginal rates as much as the variation in the provincial factors that are used to calculate provincial tax. For example, at 69% Newfoundland's factor is the highest in the country, while Saskatchewan's is among the lowest, just 50%. That difference gives Newfoundland a top combined marginal rate before provincial surtaxes that is 5.51% higher than Saskatchewan's. But at top rates, Saskatchewan's surtax adds 6.125% to its marginal rates, yielding a top marginal rate more than 0.6% higher than Newfoundland's.

1994 Provincial surtaxes and flat taxes - rates and effect on marginal rates

Taxable income →

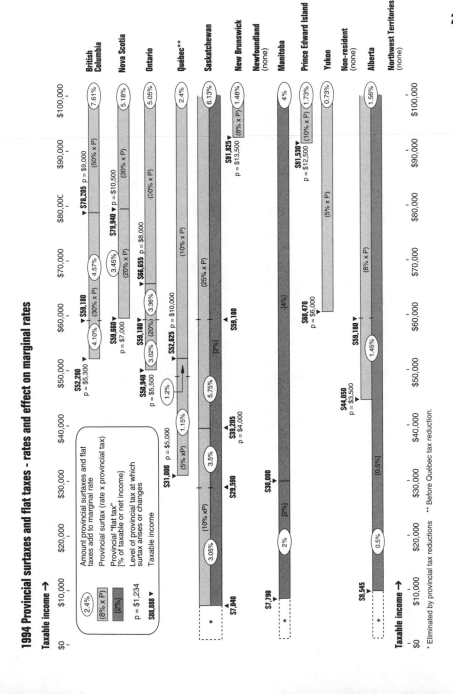

237

A5

* Eliminated by provincial tax reductions   ** Before Québec tax reduction.

Appendix 6
Credits and amounts that reduce your taxes

This appendix will help you:
• assess the value of various credits
• compare Québec credits with credits in other jurisdictions

Tax credits reduce your taxes. The second group of columns in the table shows **approximate results for jurisdictions other than Québec.** (Instead of showing a different result for each province, the table is based on provincial tax calculated as a representative factor of 55% of basic federal tax. Results for each jurisdiction will vary (see Appendix 5).

Federal credits are generally 17% of federal amounts or claims. Federal amounts are indexed annually.

Credits that apply in Québec are shown in the third group of columns. For Québec, the federal credit is, in effect, reduced by 16.5% by the Québec abatement (see Appendix 4), so that in most cases the credit drops to 14.2% of the federal amounts or claims, from the 17% (100% – 16.5%) x 17%.

Other differences for Québec residents include:

• the continued use of a deduction (rather than credits) for tuition and education expenses;

• the continued availability of credits for dependants under 18 years of age;

• no transferability of tuition fee deduction;

• supporting person may claim credit for student's post-secondary studies;

• the existence of credits for persons living alone and single parents; and

• the absence of the "equivalent-to-married" credit (apart from the federal portion).

The tax saving shown in the table (both for Québec and elsewhere) assumes that the entire credit can be used to reduce taxes. Because these credits are non-refundable, this will not be true if total credits exceed taxes otherwise payable. In that case the value of the credit is limited to the amount of tax.

Credits and amounts that reduce your 1994 taxes

	Federal amount or claim	Other than Québec — Federal credit	Other than Québec — Saving*	Québec — Credit Federal**	Québec — Credit Québec	Québec — Saving*	Special characteristics
Basic personal	$6,456	$1,098	$1,735	$917	$1,180	$2,150	Available to every taxpayer
Married	$5,380	$915	$1,445	$764	n/a	$1,971	May be reduced if income of spouse or dependant exceeds
Equivalent to married						$791	
Dependants 18 or over if infirm	$1,583	$269	$425	$225	$1,180	$1,413	
Dependants under 18 — first / each / additional		No federal credit available. See page 180 re the child tax benefit.		$520	$480		
Single parent							Québec only
Living alone				$260	$210		
Disability/mental or physical impairment	$4,233	$720	$1,137	$601	$440	$1,063	Unused portion is transferrable in some circumstances to spouse, parent, grandparent, or to child supporting a disabled parent or grandparent.
Age 65 and over	$3,482	$592	$335	$494		$952	For federal purposes, age credit is reduced above certain income levels.
Education	up to $80 per month	up to $14 per month	up to $22 per month	up to $11 per month	$330 per semester up to $660	up to $809	Outside Québec, maximum $680 is transferrable for tuition and education combined (see page 170).
Tuition fees	minimum $100 per institution				deduction	depends on marginal rate	Tuition deduction can be claimed only by the student for Québec purposes.
Pension income	up to $1,000	up to $170	up to $269	up to $142	up to $200	up to $347	
Medical expenses	over lesser of $1,614 and 3% of net income	17%	26.9%	14.2%	20%	34.7%	Not transferrable, but one spouse may claim the other's medical expenses or charitable donations (see page 171).
CPP/QPP and UI premiums	limited to maximum premium for the year	up to $349	up to $551	up to $292	up to $410	up to $692	Effective 1993, Québec's deductions for charitable donations, CPP/QPP and UI were converted into credits.
Charitable donations — first $200 / over $200	up to 20% of net income	29%	45.8%	24.2%		45%	

* The combined saving is an approximate reduction in taxes. It is calculated incorporating the federal surtax at the lower rate (3% of basic federal tax). For jurisdictions other than Québec, savings in provincial tax are approximated as 55% of the federal credit (see Appendix 5). For Québec, the saving related to the federal credit is added to the federal credit and the Québec credit to yield the combined saving.

Taxpayers whose taxable incomes exceed $62,195 pay the federal surtax at a rate of 8% of basic federal tax. Their benefit from a credit will be higher by 5% of the full federal credit (not reduced by the Québec abatement) shown in the table.

** The Québec abatement reduces the federal credit by 16.5%.

Glossary of tax abbreviations

ABIL	Allowable business investment loss
AMT	Alternative minimum tax
AVC	Additional voluntary contributions
BIL	Business investment loss
CCA	Capital cost allowance
CCPC	Canadian-controlled private corporation
CIP	Cooperative investment plan (Québec)
CNIL	Cumulative net investment loss
CPP	Canada Pension Plan
DPSP	Deferred profit sharing plan
FST	Federal sales tax
GST	Goods and Services Tax
IRA	Individual retirement account (U.S.)
MURB	Multiple-unit residential building
OAS	Old age security
PA	Pension adjustment
PSPA	Past service pension adjustment
PST	Provincial sales tax
QBIC	Québec business investment company
QPP	Québec Pension Plan
QSBC	Qualifying small business corporation
QSSP	Québec stock savings plan
RPP	Registered pension plan
RRIF	Registered retirement income fund
RRSP	Registered retirement savings plan
SBC	Small business corporation
SDI	Société de développement industriel du Québec
SIN	Social Insurance Number
UCC	Undepreciated capital cost
UI	Unemployment insurance

Price Waterhouse offices across Canada

Halifax, N.S. B3J 3N4
1801 Hollis Street
Suite 900
Telephone: (902) 420 1900
Telecopier: (902) 420 1755

Québec (Québec) G1V 4W2
Tour de la Cité (Sainte-Foy)
870 - 2600, boul. Laurier
Telephone: (418) 658 5782
Telecopier: (418) 656 6640

Montréal (Québec) H3B 2G4
1250, boul. René-Lévesque ouest
Bureau 3500
Telephone: (514) 938 5600
Telecopier: (514) 938 5709

Ottawa, Ontario K2P 2K3
Barrister House
180 Elgin Street
Suite 1100
Telephone: (613) 238 8200
Telecopier: (613) 238 4798

Toronto, Ontario M5X 1H7
1 First Canadian Place
Suite 3300
Box 190
Telephone: (416) 863 1133
Telecopier: (416) 365 8215

Toronto, Ontario M5H 3V7
20 Queen Street West
Suite 200
Box 75
Telephone: (416) 977 2555
Telecopier: (416) 977 3538

Scarborough, Ontario M1H 3C3
(Metro East Office)
1200 Markham Road
Suite 400
Telephone: (416) 439 9444
Telecopier: (416) 431 8620

North York, Ontario M2P 2B7
4110 Yonge Street
Suite 502
Telephone: (416) 222 8878
Telecopier: (416) 222 8749

Etobicoke, Ontario M9W 6V1
135 Queen's Plate Drive
Suite 400
Telephone: (416) 745 9800
Telecopier: (416) 745 2226

Mississauga, Ontario L4Z 3M3
Mississauga Executive Centre
Suite 1100
One Robert Speck Parkway
Telephone: (905) 272 1200
Telecopier: (905) 272 3937

Burlington, Ontario L7N 3J5
3380 South Service Road
Telephone: (905) 333 5050
Telecopier: (905) 333 6443

Hamilton, Ontario L8N 3R1
4 Hughson Street South
P.O. Box 1018
Telephone: (905) 525 9650
Telecopier: (905) 525 2643

Kitchener, Ontario N2G 4W1
Canada Trust Centre, Suite 900
55 King Street West
Telephone: (519) 579 6300
Telecopier: (519) 579 8701

London, Ontario N6B 3L1
Canada Trust Tower
275 Dundas Street, Suite 1500
Telephone: (519) 679 9160
Telecopier: (519) 679 1435

Windsor, Ontario N9A 6T3
Bank of Commerce Building
100 Ouellette Avenue
Suite 1200
Telephone: (519) 258 6052
Telecopier: (519) 258 5457

Winnipeg, Manitoba R3B 0X7
2200 One Lombard Place
Telephone: (204) 943 7321
Telecopier: (204) 943 7774

Regina, Saskatchewan S4P 2C2
Bank of Commerce Building
1867 Hamilton Street, Suite 1250
Telephone: (306) 757 5917
Telecopier: (306) 757 7956

Saskatoon, Saskatchewan S7K 7E6
123 - 2nd Avenue South
Suite 400
Telephone: (306) 244 6164
Telecopier: (306) 653 3813

Calgary, Alberta T2P 3V7
1200, 425 - 1st Street S.W.
Telephone: (403) 267 1200
Telecopier: (403) 233 0883

Calgary, Alberta T2W 4X9
(Calgary South Office)
10201 Southport Road S.W.
Suite 1000, Southland Plaza
Telephone: (403) 974 5300
Telecopier: (403) 258 1121

Edmonton, Alberta T5J 2Z1
1501 Toronto Dominion Tower
Edmonton Centre
Telephone: (403) 493 8200
Telecopier: (403) 428 8069

Kamloops, B.C. V2C 6P5
200 - 206 Seymour Street
Telephone: (604) 372 5551
Telecopier: (604) 372 1422

Vancouver, B.C. V6B 5A5
Price Waterhouse Centre
601 West Hastings Street
Telephone: (604) 682 4711
Telecopier: (604) 662 5300

Surrey, B.C. V3R 0N9
15127 -100th Avenue
Suite 401
Telephone: (604) 582 3400
Telecopier: (604) 582 3401

Richmond, B.C. V6X 3J6
5611 Cooney Road
Suite 100
Telephone: (604) 231 5500
Telecopier: (604) 231 5599

Index

Index